Remembering Charlotte

Remembering Char

The University of North Carolina Press   Chapel Hill and London

lotte

Postcards

from a

New South City,

1905–1950

Tryon Street, showing Skyscraper, Charlotte, N. C.   A1871

Mary Kratt & Mary Manning Boyer

© 2000
The University of North Carolina Press
Designed by Richard Hendel with Eric M. Brooks
Set in Bodoni Antiqua and Clarendon
by Eric M. Brooks
Manufactured in Hong Kong by C&C Offset Printing Company Limited
The paper in this book meets the guidelines for
permanence and durability of the Committee on
Production Guidelines for Book Longevity of the
Council on Library Resources.
Library of Congress Cataloging-in-Publication Data
Kratt, Mary Norton.
Remembering Charlotte: postcards from a New South city,
1905–1950 / Mary Kratt and Mary Manning Boyer.
p.   cm.
Includes bibliographical references (p.   ) and index.
ISBN 0-8078-2562-x (alk. paper) —
ISBN 0-8078-4871-9 (pbk.: alk. paper)
1. Charlotte (N.C.)—History—20th century—Pictorial works.
2. Charlotte (N.C.)—Social life and customs—20th century—
Pictorial works.   3. Postcards—North Carolina—Charlotte.
I. Boyer, Mary Manning.   II. Title.
F264.C4 K725   2000
975.6'7604—dc21   00-021390

04   03   02   01   00   5   4   3   2   1

*Unless otherwise credited in an illustration caption, all
postcards and the stereo view are from the collection of
Mary Manning Boyer, with the exception of the picture
of the Kratt brothers from Portland, Oregon (see Preface),
which was loaned by Mary Kratt.*

In memory of Miles Johnson Boyer *and* William Johnson Boyer

A Few of the Fine Buildings, of Charlotte, N. C.

CONTENTS

PREFACE

Postcards often tell stories. Some postcards in this book reveal where prominent citizens lived or where significant events took place. Others show ordinary people as they celebrated, posed, worked, or went about their daily business during the early 1900s. The authors' fondness for postcards embraces all of these, as well as two particular postcards which are their own families' heirlooms.

One is a picture of Mary Manning Boyer's father-in-law, Charlotte architect Martin Boyer Jr. (1893–1970), who made a historic contribution to the city when the U.S. Mint on West Trade Street was dismantled in 1933. He assisted free of charge in its reconstruction in a pasture in Eastover, where it would become the Mint Museum of Art, the first art museum in North Carolina. The Mint had been designed by an eminent American architect, William Strickland of Pennsylvania, and built in Charlotte in 1836 for the assaying and minting of gold from Charlotte's gold rush.

The other postcard is a 1910 portrait from Portland, Oregon, which shows Mary Kratt's father-in-law as a boy in stair-step order with his four brothers, two on either side of him. The postcard of the boys ages two through twelve is captioned "Citizens of Tomorrow" and was distributed by the Women's Baptist Home Mission Society of Chicago. The boys, Ted, Albert, Emil, Walt, and Ed, were sons of the Rev. Jacob Kratt, a German-born Baptist minister of the German Baptist Church in Portland. The postcard, framed and much enlarged, hangs in Kratt's Charlotte home.

Postcard of Charlotte architect Martin Boyer Jr. as a young man.

In addition to the authors' families, many people aided this project. This book would not have been possible without the help of Sarah Manning Pope. She located many of the rare postcards. Others who generously shared postcards are Wade Carmichael of the Museum of History and Hezekiah Alexander Homesite, the Lake County (Illinois) Museum and Curt Teich Postcard Archives, Lew Powell, Sarah Pope, and Mary Kratt. Jack Claiborne and Dan Morrill read the manuscript and made important suggestions. We also thank Elaine Maisner and Pamela Upton at the University of North Carolina Press for their valuable editorial assistance.

The staff of the Robinson-Spangler Carolina Room at the Public Library of Charlotte and Mecklenburg County, including curator Chris Bates, Shelia Bumgarner, Valerie Burnie, Jane Johnson, Rosemary Lands, and Pam Rasfeld, went the extra mile. Others who contributed valuable information are Jean Johnson of the Museum of the New South, Dennis Lawson of Duke Energy Archives, Charles Wagner of the Carolinas Aviation Museum, and Robin Brabham, Stewart Lillard, and Lovenia Summerville of the J. Murrey Atkins Library of the University of North Carolina at Charlotte.

Postcard of five Kratt brothers of Portland, Oregon, 1910.

We are grateful for the encouragement and shared knowledge of Norman Anderson, John A. Andross, Anne Barber, Durwood Barbour, Sylvia Dalton, Marion Ellis, Tom Franklin, Jim Kratt, Stephen Massengill, Mary Lynn Morrill, Bill Parris, Mary Louise Phillips, Dannye Romine Powell, Lew Powell, Pat Schaffer, Dennis Tucker, and Ann Boyer Wright. We thank Thomas W. Hanchett, Dan Morrill, Jack Claiborne, and others who have written recent books and reports about Charlotte, and we are grateful to all who persist in widening the pool of knowledge about this city's history.

I would leave my happy home
in

Charlotte

for you.

INTRODUCTION

Postcards are everywhere—in shops, airports, newsstands, a cafe, flea market, in your own mail-box or grandmother's attic. They are so common that you might assume that they have been around for as long as the U.S. Postal Service. No, indeed. But the illustrated postcard is such a simple idea, surely it has existed as long as photography? Not so.

Illustrated postcards in this country are only about a hundred years old. They began in Europe in the 1860s, became a novelty in the United States in the 1890s, and by the early 1900s had become extremely popular. The U.S. Postal Service had first offered plain postal cards in 1873, but *postcards* as we know them were something else entirely. Between 1907 and 1914, more than a billion illustrated postcards were manufactured.

This early era of postcard popularity exactly paralleled a startling period of growth from about 1875 to 1930—the era of the New South. Charlotte, North Carolina, was a vigorous, quintessential New South town, and the postcards collected in this book help to illustrate the evolution of the town into an ambitious New South city. You might say this book is a picture-postcard celebration of New South Charlotte.

In 1900, North Carolina was overwhelmingly rural, with only 9.9 percent of its population in cities and towns. These population centers were usually on a rail line, river, or crossroads. Turn-of-the-century Charlotte, a town surrounded by hundreds of cotton farms and cotton mills, had only 18,091 residents; its population totaled 55,268 when all of Mecklenburg County was included. The postcards reading "Watch Charlotte Grow" or flaunting the image of a skyscraper with the words "The Center of the Industrial South" not only expressed local boosterism, but were also part of a national self-promotional trend in commerce taking place in other towns and cities, particularly in the newly industrialized South following the Civil War. Since "progress" was the password of the era, citizens generally thought factory smoke and construction noise were wonderful indeed.

Between 1900 and 1920, Charlotte grew 156 percent to 46,338 residents, and Mecklenburg County had a 46 percent growth to a population of 80,695. So watching Charlotte grow was not an empty boast. These two decades marked a high growth period spurred by multiplying textile mills, textile machinery manufacture, banking, hydroelectric power, railroads, and a World War I army training camp. How did it happen that in the fifty-year period from 1880 to 1930 Charlotte grew from being an insignificant rural post–Civil War town, smaller than either Raleigh or Wilmington, to a booming city?

Part of the answer is railroads. The rail lines in place before the Civil War period had expanded remarkably to make Charlotte a transportation hub. Historian Tom Hanchett, in *Sorting Out the New South City*, writes, "Railroad connections transformed Charlotte from just another backcountry town to a place of regional importance. By 1876, lines radiated in six directions from the small city, giving it the best rail connections in the Carolinas." Rails stretched north to Richmond and beyond, south to Atlanta, and both east and west to connect to all the southeastern states. Charlotte was the meeting point of the Southern and Seaboard rail systems.

These rail corridors ran through vast cotton fields owned and tilled by hundreds of farmers. Soon, along these rail lines, villages sprang up around a cotton gin, a general store, a mule trading venture, a blacksmith shop, and a livery stable. Outlying farm villages, such as Pineville, Cornelius, and Matthews, formed at the junction of a road, a rail line, a cotton gin, and subsequently a cotton mill.

In 1881, Charlotte had one cotton mill. By 1907, 360 cotton mills lay within one hundred miles of Charlotte for spinning and knitting cotton from nearby farms. Prior to 1880, local cotton had journeyed to northern mills for creation into yarn and cloth. This revolution was no accident. Piedmont Carolina entrepreneurs, often educated in the North, combined energy, expertise, and contacts with excellent rail connections and financial acumen. They believed manufacturing would build a New South. They called it "The Cotton Mill Campaign," a vigorous, focused, up-by-the-bootstraps push to become a diverse manufacturing region rather than a purely agricultural one dependent on northern manufacture. Charlotte entrepreneur Daniel A. Tompkins lit this fire in the region, insisting that the South could manufacture anything as well as the North.

In *Independence and Empire*, Patrick J. Hearden writes that among southern leaders "almost everyone agreed that cotton mill building would spark general economic development and restore prosperity and power to the entire region."

It worked. Newspaper publisher Wade Harris in 1907 described Charlotte as "the hub of the cotton mill industry in the South. It is to Charlotte that capitalists come when they want a cotton mill built and equipped." It was also where they sent their machinery for repair, and where they often came for financing and for retail and wholesale trade. Charlotte called itself "The Electric City"—"the Centre of the greatest electric power development in the South." Tobacco tycoon James B. Duke and his brother Ben used an office on Tryon Street to organize and finance the creation of hydroelectric power for cotton mills and local towns. Such development in turn created the need for banks and other financial services. In 1907, Charlotte, with a population of about 30,000, had ten banks and savings and loan companies.

The standard manner in which these mills were usually built is analyzed by Mildred Gwin Andrews in *Men and the Mills*: "Machinery people of the East would take stock [in the new factory] for the value of the machinery, while the local people . . . would take stock for buildings and equipment. A local man who gave $10,000 capital would be elected president, another often gave the site. . . . As soon as possible the machinery company divested itself of the stock. Often a local bank would make up any balance needed." But the lessons and hardships of huge northern mills were not lost on local leaders. They worked also to diversify, to create a broad base of industries to avoid hazardous dependence on a single crop or product economy.

In *Sketches of Charlotte*, published in 1907, Wade Harris credits Charlotte leaders with familiar assertive traits which forecast the city's future character: "Charlotte does not hang back and wait for strangers to come in with their money and do things for it; it puts its money into things, shows the prospective investor what it is doing and bids him come in and do as well, or better, if he can."

Charlotte prospered. During this period, from 1880 to 1929, Charlotte welcomed many innovations that began transforming the commercial life of the region. An electric trolley system created streetcar neighborhoods in nearly every part of the city, beginning in Dilworth and spreading to Elizabeth, Piedmont Heights, Myers Park, and Eastover and to the cotton-mill villages of North Charlotte and Chadwick-Hoskins on the Westside. The city took the lead in the development of highways and became the nexus of a major roadway system that linked North and South Carolina, making Charlotte a center of commerce in both states. The city also saw the rise of its first steel-frame skyscraper, boasted the arrival of a civic auditorium and modern hotels, and built its first hospitals. To broadcast these achievements, Charlotte was a leader in the popular media: it produced the state's largest morning and afternoon newspapers, and the first radio and television stations in the Carolinas.

In keeping with the spirit of progress, Charlotte's colleges and universities advanced during this period. Johnson C. Smith University added new buildings and changed its name to honor the deceased husband of its donor, Jane Berry Smith. Presbyterian College for Women relocated from uptown Charlotte and took the name Queens College, with a spacious new campus and buildings in the prestigious Myers Park neighborhood. Davidson College was rejuvenated by the funds from the newly formed Duke Endowment announced in J. B. Duke's Charlotte mansion in the 1920s. Elizabeth College, a Lutheran college for young women, presided at the end of Elizabeth Avenue and concentrated on music education.

Uptown, Charlotte drew blue-collar and white-collar visitors from nearby towns who came to shop at the large department stores, Belk's, Efird's, and Ivey's. Many came to the "nickelodeons," those cheap, small storefront places where they crowded to watch early silent films called the "movies." And soon large movie palaces, like the Carolina Theater, drew thousands in the 1920s to the talking movies. In the 1800s, businesses needed to be in the two-block center of town to succeed. They were tightly surrounded with prestigious homes beginning in the third block from the Square. By the 1920s, businesses filled a twenty-block commercial area surrounding the Square. Between 1903 and 1929, eleven commercial buildings of seven to twenty stories were erected within four blocks of the Square.

Both banking and medical facilities concentrated in uptown Charlotte in this period. Fourth Ward contained three hospitals, as well as the Charlotte Eye, Ear, Nose, and Throat Clinic; the Charlotte Sanatorium; and the North Carolina Medical College. Hundreds of color postcards showed the high-walled financial district of South Tryon Street, dubbing it the "Wall Street of Charlotte." The Federal Reserve's imposing branch on South Tryon Street opened in 1927 to serve Carolina banks with cash reserves, rapid check clearing, and loans, and to provide coin and currency for banks.

Clearly, New South Charlotteans witnessed an impressive building boom, as documented by many of the postcards in this collection. Many of the historic buildings that remain in the center of the city today were erected during the prosperous textile and financial era of the first three decades of the twentieth century: Latta Arcade and Brevard Court, the Johnston Building, Mecklenburg Investment Company, the old City Hall and Courthouse buildings on East Trade Street, One Tryon Center (formerly First National Bank), Carolina Theater, Dunhill Hotel, Mint Museum of Craft and Design (old Montaldo's building), Ivey's Building, Spirit Square Center for the Arts (old First Baptist Church), First United Methodist Church, the Frederick and the Poplar Apartments in Fourth Ward, the east wing of the Charles R. Jonas Federal Building, and the James K. Polk Building/NC State Offices (former Coddington Building) on North Graham Street.

During and prior to the era of the postcards in this book, citizens used the term "uptown" to describe the historic center of Charlotte, those central blocks surrounding the crossroads (Square) at Trade and Tryon Streets. For this reason, and because it is sited on a ridgeline uphill from the surrounding land, the center city is termed "uptown" in postcard captions.

Among the early postcards, the most striking were those printed in Germany, where craftsman printers received American negatives of local places and sometimes hand-colored and enhanced them to show charming, vivid scenes. The outbreak of World War I prevented such imports, so subsequent cards have a different look. Rich, deep colors of sidewalk scenes with carriages, long-skirted, strolling ladies, and gentlemen in hats or caps gave way in many cases to more straightforward unpeopled views and paler tones.

Because cameras were not yet commonly available, photography in 1900 was a rare skill among North Carolinians. The Frenchman Louis Daguerre had introduced the first popular form of photography, the daguerreotype, in the 1830s, and the remarkable Civil War photographs by Matthew Brady and his associates were very familiar to southerners and northerners alike. But local pictures, particularly in a rural state such as North Carolina, were a novelty except for those by the occasional professional photographer. Charlotte's first professional, Henry Baumgarten of Baltimore, opened a studio in 1869. He took standard portraits and, as noted in a newspaper, "neatly fitted pictures in rings and lockets."

A common photographic form of the time was the stereograph view, two nearly identical photographs mounted side by side on a card and viewed through a hand-held device called a stereoscope. The device was found in many middle-class American parlors before the era of postcards, affording armchair travelers a kind of three-dimensional view of faraway places, including the famous sites and landscapes of Asia and Europe. Sometimes the photos were a pair of mischievous, comely poses of young women—attractive and fully clothed but nonetheless provocative.

The side-by-side pictures for a stereoscope scene were shot consecutively: a first picture was taken, the camera was moved the distance between the human eyes, and a second picture taken. When viewed with the stereoscope, the illusion resembles natural vision, with greater dimension and detail than a normal photograph. Oliver Wendell Holmes in 1859 marveled at these "double-eyed or twin pictures."

For a while, Americans enjoyed the stereoptic view as a refined, Victorian parlor game, but they soon fell in love with the inexpensive, versatile postcard. Postcards came at a time when numerous remarkable changes around the turn of the century—telephones, radio, movies, organized sports, and advertising—increased people's awareness of places beyond their own towns. No less fascinating was the newly invented motorcar, which enabled more Americans, now with a shorter workweek, to travel. In 1893, many flocked to the famous World's Fair in Chicago, whose extravagant Columbian Exposition dazzled travelers. Small-town Americans bragged on their Chicago adventure by sending a postcard home.

At the same time, a movement began to flourish in America in which architects and landscape planners promoted what they called "the good and beautiful city." It reflected Americans' newfound pride in urban homes, gardens, and picturesque city and village scenes. Townspeople were also proud of train stations, courthouses, city halls, parks, sports, restaurants, and their tall new buildings. And it showed on their postcards, illustrated in the early 1900s to clearly demonstrate Americans' dual interests in town and tourism.

Americans also wrote to each other. In 1900, Americans used 4 billion postage stamps. In 1922, they used far more—14.3 billion. Rural Free Delivery Service had begun in 1896, which meant that Americans who lived far from town no longer had to come miles to the nearest post office to get their mail. It would, wonder of wonders, find them! Now picture postcards could travel to remote mailboxes on a desolate country road; a farmer's wife might receive a personal note on the back of a photograph from her sister in the wider, yearned-for world.

Some postcards were the camera work of itinerant photographers. For a fee, they took photo

Working in the prepostcard era, Rufus Morgan photographed and published views of Charlotte and other parts of the United States. He made this stereoscopic card, one of the earliest photographs of Charlotte, about 1873, showing a rustic scene in the first block of North Tryon Street. Included in Morgan's photographic series, Characteristic Sketches of Southern Life, it is titled "A team peculiar to the region." A wagonload of wood is hitched to an unlikely team of three oxen and a horse, accompanied by a man on horseback. The building (left) with high porch and chimneys is the early Charlotte Hotel, next to what may have been a tavern. The "clothing" store is J. A. Young and Son, which sold "hats, caps, gents furnishing goods and umbrellas."

Next right, "Mrs. P. Query" is the millinery shop of dressmaker Query, who started her business in 1856. She also sold silk handkerchiefs, gloves, lace collars, and trims. A reporter who ventured into the hosiery section reported that he "fainted on the spot" amid a "wilderness of violets, daisies and stripes." Query's ad in 1890 invited Charlotte ladies to "Come and see the latest in what is to be worn, and how to wear it." By the late 1870s she had moved her shop to East Trade Street.

The house (far right) is that of surveyor, politician, and businessman Thomas Polk, a key player in establishing the town of Charlotte and in the move for independence in May 1775. The house had been built on North Tryon Street at East Trade Street, then moved three doors from the corner of Trade and remodeled as a tobacco factory (as pictured). His residence became known as the Cornwallis house because the British commander Lord Charles Cornwallis had headquartered here in 1780. Among Thomas Polk's furnishings were a desk and bookcase, Windsor chairs, walnut and mahogany tables, brass candlesticks, soup tureens, and silver and glass tumblers. In 1791, Polk entertained President George Washington when the president visited Charlotte and stayed in an inn across the Square. A man named George Hall bought the structure in 1880 and disassembled and moved it to the county, where he rebuilt it as a cattle barn. The Polk site is now the Bank of America and Blumenthal Performing Arts Center.

portraits of ordinary people—bride and groom, mother and child, father and son, the graduate, even an entire family in makeshift studios with drapes or period fashions and background furniture. Popular and more personal than city scenes, these were printed on heavy photographic paper with POSTCARD printed on the back, and proudly mailed to distant relatives and friends.

In 1898, the post office created a reduced rate for nonpostal-service printed postcards. Many of these were penny postcards, which cost a one-cent stamp to mail. In the novels of popular authors of the time, such as Henry James and Edith Wharton, Americans were reading about places they might never go; far more personal was a picture postcard in your mailbox with a note on the back or an arrow pointing to a hotel room on the front ("lonely!"). At first, you could write only in the white space under or beside the picture, with the entire back designated by the post office for the address. Some of the postcards in this collection display this space reserved for written messages. More and more frequently, folks began to send postcards with simple news of their travels ("We'll arrive Tuesday next on the noon train." or "You'll never believe this canyon!") and to collect them.

In this collection, many postcards featuring Charlotte were mailed from the city bearing vivid messages; others passed along personal everyday news. In 1909, one writer exclaimed, "This is how Char. looked during the convention. You should have been here, looks like Coney Island." A salesman traveling through Charlotte in 1914 wrote home on a Stonewall Hotel postcard to Mrs. Mae Cartwright, Worcester, Massachusetts: "Dear Wifie, Had dinner here. A wait of four hours for train to Belmont. Everything ok. Love to all, Bert."

A note someone wrote to a sister or friend in Shelby, North Carolina, suggested the writer had taken flowers for her to a Charlotte gravesite: "The flowers were fresh and lovely. I added a few roses and was so glad to take them for you. M.G.K." "JH" wrote in 1908 on a Charlotte postcard addressed to Miss Hazel Smith of Columbus, Ohio: "Here's one card I think you haven't in your collection." Numerous cards were sent to fill the postcard collections that became a passionate hobby for many people.

Mary Manning Boyer's father saved postcards. A lifetime resident of Williamston in eastern North Carolina, F. M. Manning was a noted Martin County historian, editor, and co-owner of the Enterprise Publishing Co., which published the Williamston *Enterprise* and the Robersonville *Weekly Herald.* He also coauthored and published three books about Martin County history.

After F. M. Manning died in 1982, Mary Manning Boyer and her sister, Sarah Pope, read through his books, photographs, and file folders about such topics as floods, crops, and local personalities, choosing which to donate to colleges or area archives. On a shelf they discovered a box they had never seen before. In it, they found a small treasure of rare postcards of Williamston.

Itinerant or storefront photographers created personal postcards, such as this one, taken in a local studio with a movable car as a prop in the early 1900s. It shows a proud grandpa with his walking cane and two barefooted boys.

The division into four political and residential wards shown on this 1875 map marks four early Charlotte neighborhoods. The four wards radiated from the Square at the town's central crossroads of Trade and Tryon Streets. The wards' names continue to be used today as neighborhood and geographic markers. The Fourth Ward, for example, includes a 1890s Victorian historic district. The Square is a common term in Charlotte for the antique crossroads (map center) where the rustic early courthouse once stood. Even then, it was not the grassy parklike square familiar to many colonial cities, but an intersection where two important roads crossed. The Square was and is the vital center of the city.

This map was published, with border advertisements for local businesses and sites (note the Opera House, lower center), to celebrate the centennial of the Mecklenburg Declaration of Independence in 1775.

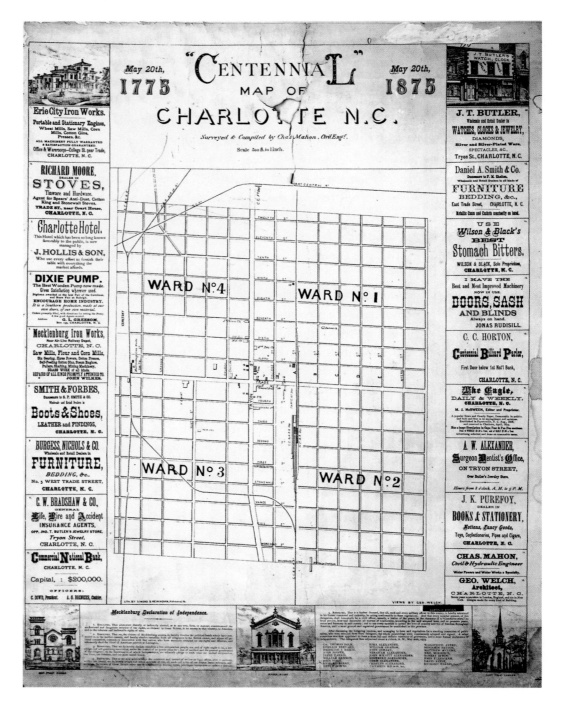

Studying the postcards, Boyer realized that early, handsomely colored cards of Charlotte, where she lived, might provide views of Charlotte not found anywhere else. Boyer became an avid collector of Charlotte and Mecklenburg County cards and a devoted local historian in her own right. Through research of her own ancestor, Hezekiah Alexander, and her documentation of historic buildings in Mecklenburg County, she tracked sources complementing her growing interest in postcards. She collected approximately 800 Charlotte postcards, as well as many cards of other locations. Her extensive Charlotte postcard collection and research on the city led to her idea for a book.

Mary Kratt's interest in Charlotte postcards derives from her fascination with turn-of-the-century Charlotte, the small, rather leisurely, New South city that existed long before she moved to North Carolina as a child in 1947. Her kin in Charlotte and Mecklenburg County included the settler families named Hood, Hunter, and Boyce. The Charlotte of Kratt's youth looked startlingly different from the city portrayed in many of the cards in Boyer's collection.

Card by card, a careful reading of this collection begins to answer our immediate questions: Who were the people who sent these postcards? Why were they here? Can we identify the buildings pictured in the cards? Spread out like a panoramic view, the postcards reveal the world of Charlotte during a period of enormous energy, growth, and ambition. They help to illustrate the building of the muscular, progressive, and modern city that Charlotte has become at the beginning of the twenty-first century. By 1998, Charlotte's city population reached 500,000, ranking it twenty-fifth in the list of fastest-growing U.S. cities.

As we compare the postcard views of Charlotte as a village and small town, with the cards showing Charlotte as it grew into a modern metropolis, we invite you to come inside the city with us. Together we'll see how these postcard images reflect the pride, energy, and immense change that transformed Charlotte into an extraordinary New South city.

Skyline, Charlotte, N. C., showing:

SOUTHERN MANUFACTURERS CLUB
FIRST PRESBYTERIAN CHURCH
SELWYN HOTEL
REALTY BUILDING
COMMERCIAL BANK BUILDING
COURT HOUSE
Y. M. C. A.

Skyline. *At the beginning of the twentieth century, the country town of Charlotte started to look like a city. This postcard trifold view postmarked 1913 shows the old century's two- and three-story brick businesses, shops with awnings, and frame houses within a few blocks of the central Square. It also reveals the new century's recent taller hotel and office buildings eastward along West Trade Street, and the distant courthouse dome (far right), different in architecture and lighter in color, reaching toward the sky.*

Cotton, railroads, hydroelectric power, and a few turn-of-the century entrepreneurs forced changes that helped make the Charlotte area the hub of the South's cotton-milling industry. With a population of 34,014 in 1910, Charlotte bridged both old and new, as seen in the horses (lower right) stabled and waiting to pull loaded wagons or to drive guests between the depot and hotels. In contrast are two buildings above the stables, the slim Commercial National Bank (1913) and the watchtower-like Tompkins Tower (1902), home of the D. A. Tompkins Machine Works at 123 South Church Street. The view from Tompkins' three-story tower atop a no-nonsense, four-story brick building was extraordinary. From a height of 150 feet, visitors watched factories and trains, horse-drawn buggies and newfangled autos, people scurrying to shops, mill villages, and farms, and in the distance Kings Mountain, Davidson College, Sharon Presbyterian Church, and, on sunny mornings, the far, faint blue silhouette of the Blue Ridge Mountains. An attendant identified the sights, while courting couples carved their names in the bricks within the tower stairs. The tower also held an interior water tank.

Downstairs, industrialist D. A. Tompkins displayed the newest cotton-mill machinery. He supplied equipment for cotton, oil, and fertilizer industries as well as sawmills, power plants, and waterworks. Tompkins was an entrepreneur, engineer, author, promoter, organizer of the Southern Manufacturers' Club (lower left), and newspaper owner. His visionary presence changed Charlotte from a farm town into the industrial center developing visibly in this postcard view.

A Few of the Fine Buildings, of Charlotte, N. C.

A few of the fine buildings. *Charlotte photographer W. M. Morse, who lived in Fourth Ward, took this postcard photograph in January 1907 from the courthouse dome across South Tryon Street. Looking northwest, it shows the dense residential-commercial mix of uptown Third Ward. In the foreground (left to right) are large typical frame homes behind the Associate Reformed Presbyterian Church, which opened at 236 South Tryon Street in 1891. To its right is the triple-massed front of the Piedmont Insurance Building, 220 South Tryon Street, housing offices and King's Business College in 1909; the tall ornate facade of the Southern States Trust Co. and, inside it, the Academy of Music; the 4 C's Building (Charlotte Consolidated Construction Co., which originally built and owned the streetcar system and developed Dilworth neighborhood). To the far right is the turreted YMCA. In the upper right, find the spire of First Presbyterian Church. Then to its left is the jutting, square Tompkins Tower designed by architects Oliver D. Wheeler and Neil Runge, which stood until 1942. Next left in the horizon's center is the cylindrical water standpipe at Graham and Fifth Streets. Farther left, just above the A.R.P. church spire, locate the low, red-brick, boxy tower of the early federal post office beside the U.S. Mint.*

View from Tompkins Tower. *If you were to perch on top of the tallest building in town about 1905–1920, what would you see? Look east, north, west, and south. A photographer commissioned by a commercial postcard company took basic shots to show Charlotte's center, the hazy perimeter, and the countryside just beyond the town. These would include, far or near, almost every town dweller's workplace, church, neighborhood, and possibly his or her home.*

Skyline, showing City Hall, Realty Building, and Selwyn Hotel. *Before 1908, the prime camera perch was the slender, red-brick Tompkins tower. The tower's nearest rival was the standpipe at Fifth and Graham Streets, but taking a photo from the iron ladder up its side was as precarious as clinging to the needle spire of First Presbyterian Church. What is quite clear from these postcards is the close mix of industry and handsome housing.*

BIRD'S-EYE VIEW, LOOKING NORTH, CHARLOTTE, N. C.

Skyline showing bird's-eye view looking north. *This postcard shows the tall stepped gables, brown stone walls, tower, and weathervane of City Hall, the Second Presbyterian Church, and First Baptist Church, behind which are the smokestacks of North Charlotte's large textile mills. The smoke signaled "Charlotte's Industrial Heart" beside the major rail artery paralleling Tryon Street.*

Bird's Eye View, Tryon Street, Charlotte, N. C.

Bird's-eye view, Tryon Street looking north across the Square *(south face of Realty/ Independence Building). This was the best way to photograph the skyscraper because its builders put a capstone on only two sides.*

LOOKING WESTWARD, FROM THE REALTY BUILDING, CHARLOTTE, N. C.

Realty Building, Charlotte, N. C.

Looking westward from the Realty Building. *This view shows the* Selwyn Hotel (right foreground) *and West Trade Street.*

Granite Row. *Mercantile prosperity has always depended on traffic and people coming to buy. The five three-story buildings at the Square (southwest corner) called Granite Row, were built in 1850–51 to profit from the coming of the railroad to Charlotte and its linkage to seaports and to the Northeast. In this picture postmarked 1911, the buildings (beginning with Blake's Drugstore, center and left to green building with awning) housed jewelers, millinery shops, a bank, and a tea room at street level with residences above. Some of the facades were remodeled from 1909 to 1919 by Louis Asbury Sr. These were among the first brick or granite-type commercial buildings replacing typical wood frame which had been built when Charlotte's population was about 1,000. Note the sign at the roof cornice, "Get Right With God." The last of these row buildings survived until May 3, 1987. It was originally the silversmith shop of Thomas Trotter and became a Charlotte-Mecklenburg Historic Landmark in 1985.*

South Tryon Street *(not Tyson, as on the card).*
Charlotte's original main street, Tryon, was the
ridgeline artery named for Royal Governor
William Tryon of England, who governed North
Carolina (1765–71) under King George III.
Beyond the few blocks of uptown commercial
buildings around the Square (circa 1900), the
street was residential and looked like this on both
ends of Tryon Street. Note the trolley tracks, farm
wagons, carriages, snow, mud, and sidewalks.
Postmarked 1907.

Tryon Street

Tryon Street, showing Skyscraper, Charlotte, N. C.

A1871

Tryon Street showing skyscraper

Charlotte's two skyscrapers

North Tryon Street

(not Tyson Street, as printed on card)

North Tryon Street

Charlotte, N.C.   North Tryon Street.

Representative business block

Representative Business Block, showing New American Trust Co. Building and Academy of Music, Charlotte, N. C.

View of Tryon Street, looking south

Charlotte, N. C., View of Tryon Street,
Looking South from Seventh Street.

South Tryon Street

South Tryon Street,
Charlotte, N. C.

SOUTH TRYON STREET FROM SQUARE, CHARLOTTE, N. C.

South Tryon Street from the Square

TRYON STREET, LOOKING SOUTH, CHARLOTTE, N. C.

Tryon Street, looking south

Independence Square, looking north

Independence Square, looking south

TRADE STREET VIEWS

West Trade Street, looking east

West Trade Street

5906-29

Trade Street, looking west

East Trade Street *(not West Trade, as printed on the card)*

ROCK HOUSE, CHARLOTTE, N. C.—3

Hezekiah Alexander Stone House. *Charlotte's earliest remaining dwelling from colonial days is the stone house of Hezekiah and Mary Alexander (1774). This card shows an added twentieth-century porch which was removed when the neglected house was restored in 1950 by local chapters of the Daughters of the American Revolution. The work was aided by contributions from citizens and members of the Hezekiah Alexander family. The Hezekiah Alexander Foundation completed a major restoration in the 1970s. Alexander was a prominent Scots-Irish Presbyterian landowner, justice of the peace, elected official, and college trustee. When the Fifth Provincial Congress was called to establish a permanent government for the state, Alexander was a delegate and served on the committee drafting the N.C. State Constitution and Bill of Rights. He was a leader in the May 1775 movement for independence from Great Britain. The home is a popular, outstanding house museum listed on the National Register of Historic Places. It became a Charlotte-Mecklenburg Historic Landmark in 1975.*

OLD PHIFER HOME.
CHARLOTTE. N C.

Phifer House. *This solid, elegant, historic home once stood in the 700 block of North Tryon Street. Built by William Fulenwider Phifer in 1852, it was used as headquarters by Confederate general P. G. T. Beauregard. Best remembered are the events of April 22–26, 1865, when the entire Confederate Cabinet and Jefferson Davis met in Charlotte. Crucial decisions concerning the war's end had to be made in the meetings, but Secretary of the Confederate Treasury George Trenholm was too ill to leave the guest room's four-poster bed. The cabinet met upstairs in this house in the final days of the Confederacy.*

The vacant house was boarded up for twenty years and fell into such serious disrepair that it was demolished in 1943. One owner had remodeled it, adding bay windows and other decorations in the popular Queen Anne style. Originally, the Phifer place covered extensive acreage and had numerous outbuildings, including slave quarters and a carriage house. Phifer's slaves made bricks for the house and free-standing kitchen. The house, designed by a Philadelphia architect, had a wide central hall and nine rooms furnished with Empire mahogany furnishings made in Philadelphia. A Sears Roebuck store was located on the site and was later adapted to become the Harold R. Marshall County Services Center.

Residence of Genl. Stonewall Jackson, Charlotte, N. C.

13417

Mrs. Stonewall Jackson's residence

(not the general's home, as stated on the card).
As the city's most celebrated woman, Mary Anna
Morrison Jackson was known as "The First Lady
of Charlotte." General Jackson never lived in
Charlotte, but his wife was a native, born in
1831 at 2500 Derita Road. After the death of her
husband, Mrs. Jackson returned to her home in
Lincoln County, then moved back to Charlotte
when her daughter Julia became a student at
Charlotte Female Institute. She purchased a home
at 507 West Trade Street. Here she received
elderly soldiers visiting Charlotte by train. Her
home occupied the second lot east of the train
station, according to a 1900 Sanborn Insurance
map. A new station was constructed in 1905
next door to her residence.

Mrs. Stonewall Jackson's Residence, Charlotte, N.C.

Mrs. Stonewall Jackson's residence.

In 1907, Mrs. Jackson moved two blocks toward
the center of town to 306 West Trade Street,
close to her church, First Presbyterian, where her
father, Robert Hall Morrison, had served as
minister. Locals recall she kept her late husband's
saddle on the newel post in her front hall.
The Morrison family was accustomed to social
prominence: Mrs. Jackson's father had been the
first president of Davidson College, and two of
her sisters also married Confederate generals. As
Charlotte's grande dame, Mrs. Jackson received
visits from several U.S. presidents who came to
call. She died in 1915; her home was demolished
about 1925 and was replaced by the Builders
Building, renamed the Peace Building in 1986.

Charlotte residence of Z. B. Vance. *The exceptional storyteller and wit, a three-time governor, congressman, and U.S. senator, Zebulon Baird Vance (1830–94) was called "Zeb" by his beloved constituents and friends. Mountain folk claimed him, for he was born and practiced law in Buncombe County. Statesville claimed him because he had a home and family there. After the Civil War ended in 1865, Vance formed a law partnership in Charlotte and practiced with Clement Dowd until 1876. His Charlotte home, pictured here, sat at the corner of East Sixth and A Streets. A Street ran parallel to the Carolina Central Railroad track. When he lived in this house with its picket fence and tall oaks, his wife was an invalid. A slender granite marker near the former homesite describes Vance briefly. A beloved leader in tumultuous times, he was imprisoned in Washington at the close of the Civil War for having been the war governor of North Carolina. His passion was politics. In 1892, he told a senator, "Charlotte is the biggest town for its size in the South."*

Grounds of A. Steinhauser. *Memories of his youth perhaps prompted Alois Steinhauser to create an unusual sylvan pleasure ground on his four acres on Derita Road. Certainly Charlotte knew nothing else like it in 1903, when Steinhauser purchased four acres for $800 on a promontory one and a half miles north of town. Born in Austria in 1851, Steinhauser immigrated to the United States via Philadelphia in 1891. In 1902 he was an agent for the Carolina Sizing Co., a textile-related business, and by 1910 he was proprietor. The grounds and vistas he created included (as pictured) a deer park, a fountain encircled by native stonework, a gazebo, and benches. For rustic, farm-oriented Mecklenburg County, his was a sophisticated idea that preceded any city-owned park. He sold the property in 1912 to F. O. Hawley Jr. for $10,000. The general area became Graham Heights suburb, and Derita Road near its intersection with West 26th Street became North Graham Street. (Postmarked 1912).*

Beautiful Residences, Charlotte, N. C.
O. A. Robbins.

Beautiful Residences, Charlotte, N. C.
F. O. Hawleys Jr.

O. A. Robbins and Hawley residences. *The lady of the Robbinses' grand plantation-style home, which had been built by 1905 and called "Belle Air," was a native of New Orleans, Olivia Barthelemy Robbins. A business-woman as well as a hostess, she also built several apartment houses in Dil-worth. She and her husband, Oliver A. Robbins, their children, and her mother lived at 1211 East Boulevard. Tragedy struck the family in 1897, when their six-year-old son, Felix, was swept away in the surf and drowned near their cottage at Carolina Beach. In 1898, Mr. Robbins owned a Dilworth company which made braided window-sash cords, clotheslines, and yarn, and also sold cotton-mill machinery and equipment. He is listed as an architect in the 1911 City Directory with his company, O. A. Robbins, Co. In 1902 he was also agent for the noted Frick Co. of Pennsylvania, providing heavy machinery, engines, and repairs. Apartments were later added to each side of the mansion and it was called the Valeda Mansion apartments, named for Mrs. Robbins's mother, Valeda. The home is no longer standing.*

The Hawley residence is described on page 33.

The New Hawley Residence.

Home of Stuart V. Cramer.

Charlotte, N. C.

Home of R. O. Alexander.

HEATHCOTE, CHARLOTTE, N. C.

Heathcote. *One of Charlotte's grand turn-of-the-century mansions was not in the center of town, as most imposing homes were. It was built at Central and Louise Avenues by Benjamin Dawson Heath, a developer of the area known as Piedmont Park. Heath also organized and served as president of Charlotte National Bank, with extensive interests in cotton mills, insurance companies, railroads, and the Charlotte Speedway. Twice married and the father of sixteen children, he needed a big house. Heathcote was designed in Colonial Revival style by Charlotte architect Frank P. Milburn in 1899 and built soon after. It is no longer standing. (Postmarked 1906.)*

opposite

Home of Stuart Warren Cramer (left). *At 301 East Morehead Street, engineer Cramer (1868–1940) built his large, shingled Victorian winter home about 1897 and called it Withgate Hall. His summer home of stone sat atop Cramer Mountain near Cramerton Mills which he headed. Cramer had come to Charlotte as assayer at the Charlotte Mint (1889–93), but he is best known for his patented inventions in textile machinery, especially as a pioneer in the field of humidifying and air conditioning and as a planner and equipper of numerous southern cotton mills. His Charlotte company Parks-Cramer Co. produced "Controlled Climate" equipment to aid in producing quality cotton cloth and yarn. Neighbors on East Morehead Street recall Cramer's Chinese male servants who exercised on the parallel bars at the public school across the street and were much admired by gawking schoolchildren. The Charlotte Country Day School began in this Cramer house and later moved to a temporary Selwyn Avenue location. The house was demolished in the 1950s.*

Hawley House (above right). *This is one of the finest examples of the neoclassical revival style, built in 1906–7 by wealthy cotton merchant H. K. McKinnon for his daughter Elizabeth McKinnon Hawley. The home was designed by architect Leonard L. Hunter and shows the grand residential style typical of the neighborhood at 923 Elizabeth Avenue, just seven blocks down East Trade Street from the Square. Elizabeth's*

husband, Francis O. Hawley Jr., became a prominent pharmacist. Before its demolition in 1990, the house was a boarding house known as "The Clary" and in the 1930s was Mrs. Morehead's boarding house where $7.50 a week bought two meals daily. Later a dentist called it home and built his street-level offices in front. It became the Edmor Motor Inn in 1964 and was designated a Charlotte-Mecklenburg Historic Landmark in 1990.

R. O. Alexander Home (below right). *Still standing in the New South streetcar neighborhood of Dilworth ("The City of Avenues"), this striking Colonial Revival house was built in 1900–1901 for the prominent owner of a roofing/paving company and a brick-making company, John L. Villalonga. No expense was spared in the home's fine workmanship; its expansive two and half stories, long front porch, and porte cochere were designed by architect C. C. Hook, who specialized in Colonial Revival style. Villalonga sold his showplace home at 301 East Park Avenue in 1903 to R. O. Alexander and moved to New York City. Alexander was a wealthy cotton broker and a Presbyterian evangelist who conducted revivals, proclaiming that material success would come to those who converted to his beliefs. In 1948, fire consumed the home's interior core, which was repaired. It later became a boarding house before being handsomely restored. It was designated a Charlotte-Mecklenburg Historic Landmark in 1979. At the close of the twentieth century, the Villalonga-Alexander house is the largest remaining private residence in Dilworth.*

Brevard Nixon Home. *Brevard Nixon lived with his family at 803 South Tryon Street, an auspicious address among other large houses. His home reflects his position as a prominent attorney with the firm McCall and Nixon and after 1905 in an independent practice. A native of Catawba Springs in Lincoln County, Nixon had been a teacher and newspaper editor before becoming a Charlotte lawyer in 1895. The home is no longer standing. (Postmarked 1912.)*

Residence of Brevard Nixon, Lawyer, 803 South Tryon St. Charlotte, N. C.

R. M. Miller Jr. residence. *This imposing home at 406 North Tryon Street announced the prominence of Robert Morrison Miller Jr., a wealthy and prominent Charlotte textile industrialist, bank officer, and one-time president of the American Cotton Manufacturers Association. The mansion was built in 1909. A formal invitation card from the Miller family in 1916 announces dancing to begin at nine o'clock, December 25, at their residence. After Miller's death in 1925, the house was briefly a dining facility called Mayfair Manor. In 1929, J. M. Harry and Co. funeral home rented the house. In 1938, it became the Harry and Bryant Funeral Home. It is the oldest surviving funeral firm in the city. The elegant building at the northeast corner of Seventh and North Tryon Streets was razed in 1949.*

Charlotte, N. C. - Industrial Center of the New South - Residence of R. M. Miller, Jr.

Home of Mr. E. D. Latta

Home of Mr. C.W. Tillett

Mr. R.A. Dunn's Residence   Beautiful Homes of Charlotte, N.C.

Home of Edward Dilworth Latta (top). *The grand six-columned, white mansion with porte cochere announced the position and wealth of its owner. Latta built it on Charlotte's new electric-streetcar line, which he owned, in the elegant new suburb named Dilworth, which he also owned and developed. This house was under construction in 1902 and stood near the end of the trolley line at 600 East Boulevard. It had a ball room, Tiffany glass, rich paneling, ceiling paintings, and a Ben Hur mural on the landing. Known for his vision and philanthropy, Latta was a prime mover in early-twentieth-century Charlotte. The home was later used by Holy Trinity Greek Orthodox Church. The new cathedral built next door was consecrated in 1954. When the house was demolished in 1966, it was replaced by the Hellenic Community Center and education building.*

Home of C. W. Tillett (middle). *This Greek Revival residence of prominent attorney Charles W. Tillett Sr. was built in the 1890s at 801 North Tryon Street at the corner of Eleventh Street, across the side street from the First A.R.P. Church. Tillett had a law practice in Charlotte by 1892 and lived in this house from about 1897 until his death in 1936. He wrote notable publications, one pleading for religious tolerance. He served as president of the North Carolina Bar Association. His wife, Carrie, was a prominent local and statewide civic leader. After the home's demolition, an A&P market occupied the corner site, closing in 1975 as the last uptown A&P in Charlotte.*

R. A. Dunn's residence (bottom). *Built in the early 1900s at 511 North Tryon Street, this was the home of one of the city's most successful business and church leaders. Robert Dunn was a partner in Burwell and Dunn, which in 1945 was said to be the oldest surviving Charlotte mercantile business. Earlier, he was president of Commercial National Bank and the Highlands Hotel Co., president of the Davidson College Board of Trustees in 1929, and moderator in 1931–32 of the General Assembly of the Presbyterian Church in the U.S. By 1955, the home was no longer listed in the City Directory as the Dunn residence. After his death in 1945, his wife, Adele Brenizer Dunn, became president of Burwell and Dunn.*

P4964   Entrance to Myers Park, Charlotte, N. C.   Photo Underwood & Underwood, N. Y.

P4961   Myers Park, Charlotte, N. C.   Photo Underwood & Underwood, N. Y.

Myers Park Entrance. *Note the iron trolley tracks leading through this gate at the intersection of Fourth Street, Hawthorne Lane, and Queens Road. The electric trolley came down East Trade Street from town onto Hawthorne Lane to enter a prestigious new streetcar neighborhood opened in 1912. Developed by George Stephens on the land of his father-in-law, John Springs "Jack" Myers, the residential area transformed 1,100 acres of a former cotton farm and additional parcels. The Stephens Co. also built the tracks and the covered waiting stations at key stops along the grand boulevard of Queens Road. Stone for the waiting stations came from granite quarries in Winnsboro, South Carolina. The winning entry in a local contest to name the boulevard suggested it be called Queens Road. Myers Park included Horner Military School for boys and Queens College for women near the end of the trolley line. Handsome homes and landscaping gradually filled in the route, which Charlotteans considered to be far in the country. The trolley used the median, which remains the full length of Queens Road, then continued onto what later became Queens Road East, across what became the Myers Park Country Club golf course and up to the Horner School. The center entrance building was later removed for street widening. No trolley tracks were ever laid on Queens Road West, which was developed later. The waiting station became a Charlotte-Mecklenburg Historic Landmark in 1981.*

Hermitage Court and Gateway. *Real estate company owner Floyd M. Simmons had excellent contacts. He lived in the Vance Apartments at 17 Mint Street and, in November 1910, had just completed a victorious season as coach of Davidson College's football team. That year Davidson beat the University of North Carolina. From then on, he concentrated on real estate; in 1912 he developed Hermitage Court, a version of Charlotte's "suburban White Way," on a small street right up against the larger development of Myers Park. The gates were identical to those of Myers Park, the one pictured here being the West Gate and a block away being the East Gate. The house pictured at 625 Hermitage Court is Simmons's own, which dwarfed the other homes on the street. Two Scotsmen from Aberdeen fashioned the stonework on the gates and others in Myers Park. The Charlotte Observer reported that these were designed to resemble the entrance gates to Andrew Jackson's "Hermitage" near Nashville. Jackson, born near Charlotte, was a local hero as well as U.S. president. The Simmons home and gateways are still standing. The Hermitage Court gateways were designated Charlotte-Mecklenburg Historic Landmarks in 1981.*

P4948   "Harwood" suburban home of Mr and Mrs. Ralph
VanLandingham in Chatham Estates. Charlotte, N. C.   Photo Underwood & Underwood, N. Y.

P4958   Residence of Ab. V. Harrill. Myers Park.
Charlotte, N. C.   Photo Underwood & Underwood, N. Y.

Harwood. *When Ralph and Susie Harwood VanLandingham built this expansive but unpretentious Bungalow-style house in 1913, their address at 2010 The Plaza was out in the country. With five acres of gardens and grounds, they were in the new suburb of Chatham Estates near the Charlotte Country Club. The bungalow was a popular house style of the era with shingle siding, wide verandahs, and stone chimneys, designed for them by Charles C. Hook and Willard G. Rogers. The family planted hundreds of rhododendrons, roses, and shrubs among imported marble birdbaths, fountains, and benches. In the garage they kept a seven-passenger Packard to drive uptown or to their summer home in Linville. Ralph Sr. was an affluent cotton broker and Susie had owned and run the Majestic Hotel in Atlanta. In Charlotte, she became an exceptional leader, humanitarian, and world traveler. The home is on the National Register of Historic Places. It became a Charlotte-Mecklenburg Historic Landmark in 1977.*

Residence of Albert Vance Harrill. *Harrill was vice president of Southern Public Utilities Co., which later merged with Duke Power. He became supervisor of the utility's branches in numerous Piedmont Carolina cities. This home stood at 1422 Queens Road near Pembroke Avenue.*

Residence of J. L. Station, Charlotte, N. C.

Residence of J. L. Staten. *The postcard company misspelled the homeowner's name, but the house at 322 Hawthorne Lane is best known as International House. Begun in 1911 by Blythe and Isenhour builders, the house was completed in 1912 when James Lloyd Staten Sr. and his wife Lillian moved in. The Statens lived here until 1938. In 1922, Staten was president of J. L. Staten Co., a women's apparel store at 209–11 West Trade Street. He was also part owner of Little Long Co. (mercantile), and secretary of Southeastern Land Co. In the 1950s, former U.S. Ambassador to Brazil Herschel V. Johnson lived here. Subsequently the residence became a funeral home from 1959 until 1986. St. John's Baptist Church nearby purchased the home and became a major sponsor of International House, a program center which promotes friendship and understanding for visitors and newcomers from foreign countries.*

RES OF J.L. SNYDER, PINEHAVEN, N.C.

Residence of J. A. Holmes. *Jefferson A. Holmes proudly addressed this postcard of his family's rural Park Road home to friends in Benning-ton, New Hampshire. He wrote New Year's greetings reporting, "We are all well. . . . A picture of our home." The Holmeses had purchased their Mecklenburg County land for $550 in 1902 on the west side of Park Road. Note the neat cottage's detailed gable and porch, the shutters, the adult with his bicycle, the family horse and carriage (left), a front railing for tying a visitor's horse, the granite stepping block for dismounting, and the outbuildings which no doubt included a wellhouse and barn. Folks typically wore their Sunday best for photos. Holmes, his wife Elva, and mother-in-law, Elvira Adams, lived here in 1920. All were natives of New Hampshire, which was the destination of this postcard. The home is no longer standing.*

Residence of J. L. Snyder. *Architect Martin E. Boyer Jr. designed this sophisticated home for J. Luther Snyder (1873–1957), founder of the first Coca-Cola bottling plant in the Carolinas. Snyder began work as manager in Charlotte in 1902 and later owned a chain of ten Carolina bottling plants. The Snyder residence at 1901 Queens Road was located in a dense pine grove and was named Pinehaven. There is no North Carolina town by that name, as stated on the postcard. The 1923 house is of Georgian design, which Boyer enriched with handsome detail: roof slates that were proportionately smaller toward the roof line, and shutters with a stylized LS, the owner's initials. Massachusetts-trained landscape architect E. S. Draper provided the grounds' design, as he did with many Myers Park homes. Garden boxwoods in a walled rear garden comple-mented Boyer's front terrace with balustrade and the elegant, sweeping steps at the sidewalk entry. In 1957, the Irwin Belks gave the home to Queens College for use as Carol Hall, and in the 1980s it was sold to become Charlotte's most elegantly situated residential condominiums, tripled in size by adjacent buildings replicating Boyer's design.*

J. B. Duke Villa (top) **and Fountain** (bottom).

Certainly the largest and most historically important house in Charlotte is the home of James Buchanan Duke, who transformed the tobacco industry in America and financed pioneering hydroelectric power for homes and textile mills in the Carolinas. Duke (1856–1925) owned other grand mansions in the Northeast, but during his ownership of this one in his native North Carolina from 1919 until his death in 1925, he made enormous contributions. The ongoing Duke Endowment benefiting colleges, Duke University, and hospitals was founded here in 1924. Built in 1915 in the new neighborhood of Myers Park (not Meyers, as printed on the postcard), this elegant Colonial Revival house was tripled in size when Duke bought it as Lynnwood in 1919 and hired architect C. C. Hook for the job. The postcard view of the 45-room, 12-bath expanded home shows a side elevation. The stairs lead down to a 15-acre garden which had four fountains. The fountain pictured flumed 150 feet with water piped in from the Catawba River. (A home on Ardsley Road now occupies the fountain site.) Later called White Oaks, the Duke home was owned by a series of prominent Charlotte families. Renovated again, White Oaks opened in April 1998 as an executive conference center and home for the William States Lee III Leadership Institute. The elegant 50-room, 22,000-square-foot mansion operated by the Lynnwood Foundation is located at 400 Hermitage Road. It is on the National Register of Historic Places and became a Charlotte-Mecklenburg Historic Landmark in 1977.

J. B. Duke Villa in Beautiful Meyers Park, Charlotte, N. C.—28

The Wonder Fountain, J. B. Duke Estate, Meyers Park, Charlotte, N. C.—29

Tulips in Bloom,
Gardens of J. B. Ivey,
Charlotte, N. C.

"Tulips in Bloom." *One of Charlotte's important spring rituals drew thousands of visitors to the abundant, colorful tulip gardens at the home of merchant Joseph Benjamin Ivey at 1638 East Morehead Street. This 1939 photograph of twins Catherine and Josephine Medlock shows the girls dressed in Dutch attire in front of an ornamental windmill. It was reproduced as a popular postcard of Charlotte. Ivey opened the gardens each spring to the public in an era when such visual opulence was rare. In 1940, 10,000 visitors viewed 35,000 tulips. One Charlottean who came as a child to visit the Iveys not only remembers the gardens but was also impressed that the residence's guest bathroom had lavender fixtures.*

"CARNEGIE COURT," Charlotte, N. C.

Blandwood Apartments, Charlotte, N. C.

Carnegie Court. *In 1906, this handsome residence called Carnegie Court faced an interior open court formed at the rear of the original Carnegie Public Library. The back of this building faced East Sixth Street, an unusual arrangement. The building's owner was enterprising George Stephens, who would develop Myers Park in 1911. Stephens had lived earlier in one of the two apartments here, and in 1907 he rented nine rooms to members of the Lamb's Club. Several of the ten members became prominent. For example, two would be presidents of Duke Power: Norman Cocke, for whom Lake Norman is named, and E. C. Marshall, for whom Marshall Steam Plant is named. Club member David Ovens of the J. B. Ivey Co. was the namesake for Ovens Auditorium. Ovens was an influential figure in Charlotte for fifty years. Stephens asked permission of library trustees to beautify the open courtyard with grass, flowers, and shrubs, as it was visible from North Tryon Street by a narrow lane on the library's south side called Wadsworth Place. The residence became a medical building in the 1920s. The Public Library of Charlotte and Mecklenburg County expanded onto the site in 1956. A later and larger main library building now occupies the site extending to the corner of Sixth and North Tryon Streets.*

Blandwood Apartments. *On property owned as far back as 1877 by the Morehead family, John M. Morehead II and John Paul Lucas Sr. built the substantial, commodious Blandwood Apartments in 1914. The 911 South Tryon Street location was near the southeast corner at East Morehead Street. Thirty-two apartments in the three-story building, some with three bedrooms, housed a procession of Charlotte's most prominent families. The building's name was perhaps borrowed from the 1844 Greensboro mansion built by Governor John M. Morehead, who was the first president of the N.C. Railroad and grandfather of Charlotte's J. M. Morehead II. Greensboro's Blandwood still stands, but Charlotte's Blandwood Apartments were torn down in 1960.*

CHARLOTTE, N. C.   Dowd Apartments   5082

Dowd Apartments. *Industrialist W. Frank Dowd built the Dowd Apartments in 1905 at the west corner of East Morehead Street and South Boulevard. Costing about $50,000, the ten apartments were located between Charlotte's center and the new neighborhood of Dilworth, and overlooked the streetcar line at this fashionable address. The three-story structure was razed in 1954. Dismantled bricks were reused in a Myers Park home at 2300 Sherwood Avenue.*

COLONIAL APARTMENTS, CHARLOTTE, N. C.

Colonial Apartments. *With so many grand mansions along North Tryon Street in the early 1900s, fortunate indeed were those who lived in apartments such as these built in 1914 at 524 North Tryon Street at the corner of Ninth Street. Architect Adlai Osborne designed the 84' × 80' structure to have sixty rooms totaling twelve apartments. The three-story brick building appears to have had a porch and corner exposure in each unit, creating cross ventilation in the days long before air conditioning. According to the City Directory, the building stood until 1967. In 1968 the site held a gas station.*

3. Leisure Time *Entertainment, Clubs, Recreation, Parks, Sports*

13410—Country Club, Charlotte, N. C.

Charlotte Country Club. *On the rustic, raised porch covered in honeysuckle and Virginia creeper, early club members enjoyed rocking chairs and hammocks. Inside they dined by massive rock fireplaces. Since the first log clubhouse was two miles west of the city limits near the Mount Holly Road, the club offered transportation from the club stable of fifteen horses and buggies and a six-seat passenger bus. From its hillside, the clubhouse overlooked Stewart's Pond on the former Wilson farm and the distant "field golf" links. Stray golf balls occasionally hit passersby on the road, and one young golfer hit the side of a cow. Before golf, members were content with card games, picnics, boating, fishing, ice skating, and dining. The gathering place was known initially as the Mecklenburg Club, organized in 1899. In one daring feat, Osmond Barringer, Charlotte's first automobile dealer, drove his car across an icy Stewart's Pond.*

In May 1910, members purchased a new 219-acre site north of the city from W. D. Rock, which included a large, handsome brick residence known as the Rock House. The house was remodeled and the original nine-hole golf course was built. In 1917, the name was changed from Mecklenburg Country Club to Charlotte Country Club. George Stephens, developer of Myers Park, had competed with Paul Chatham, developer of Chatham Estates [The Plaza], hoping to persuade the club to relocate to Myers Park, but Chatham's very liberal offer included greens construction and extension of the trolley line from Central Avenue, providing three trollies an hour to and from the Square.

After Charlotte enjoyed the 1920s decade of exceptional prosperity spurred by textile and financial growth, this new clubhouse, designed by Aymar Embury II of New York City, opened in 1931 on the Rock farm site off Mecklenburg Avenue and is still in use today.

Block showing Y.M.C.A. and Trust Bldg., in Charlotte, N.C.

North State Club (building on right). *Members of what is said to be Charlotte's oldest club, organized in 1884, met in this structure on the southwest corner of Tryon and Fourth Streets. In 1902 it had seventy-two members who paid $1.50 monthly dues. Described as an "aristocratic institution," the roster read like a who's who of professional and commercial Charlotte. New members paid a $5 initiation fee, but inventors Thomas A. Edison and E. Howard received honorary memberships in 1890. The club met at the Southern Express Co. building, erected in the 1890s.*

MYERS PARK COUNTRY CLUB, CHARLOTTE, NORTH CAROLINA   C-288-914

Myers Park Country Club. *When the Horner Military School sold its campus and buildings in 1920 to the Stephens Co., the property soon became the Myers Park Country Club, which was organized in 1921 with 350 Charlotte men as charter members. The early clubhouse (pictured) temporarily used this former administration building of the defunct Horner School before building a new clubhouse and golf course. Golf-related subdivisions were a new idea in the South, and the club's presence with approximately seventy-nine acres north of Briar Creek was a stimulus to the neighborhood. Soon the Stephens Co. loaned $15,000 toward four clay tennis courts, a swimming pool, and golf course. Landscaper Earle Draper accompanied golfer Paul Haddock, an Englishman, to lay out the first nine holes. The expanded course and club are located at 2415 Roswell Avenue.*

Charlotte, N. C., View of City Hall.

Elks Club and Colonial Club *(left of tall-steepled City Hall).*
The northeast corner of Tryon and Fifth Streets was home to two
prominent men's clubs: first the Elks in 1899–1903, then the
Colonial Club, 1904–12. This unusual Charlotte building was
designed by Frank P. Milburn, whose original plan had a corner
turret. In 1902, the Elks lodge quarters upstairs had "20 rooms
perfectly furnished," and members paid annual dues of $24.
Street level was for commerce; first a plumbing company, and
later Atkinson and Stowes Druggist and Pharmacy, occupied
the space. A large, antlered elk's head, fastened to the third-
floor corner, surveyed passersby. The Colonial Club made news
in 1909 when a gas leak started a closet fire. The building
sustained extensive damage but was later repaired. In 1910
the North Carolina Supreme Court overturned a lower court
verdict which found the Colonial Club guilty of having and
selling whisky in violation of Prohibition laws. Attorney for the
club was member Cameron Morrison, a savvy politician and
teetotaler who was later elected governor of North Carolina
(1921–25).

Southern Manufacturers' Club. *In 1910, the influential men's business and social club built this brick, marble-trimmed structure at 300 West Trade Street, across the side street (North Poplar Street) from First Presbyterian Church. It had four stories and a basement. Membership was by invitation only to an elite enclave, where northern and southern manufacturers could meet, trade, buy, and sell, often "getting up a new factory." Besides the finest ballroom in town, the club building also contained parlors, billiards, dining and guest rooms, and bachelors' quarters on the top floor. William Gorrell, a former slave, presided memorably over the cloakroom. In the library, a prized nine-foot-tall case clock bore an inscription to the SMC "given by its Northern friends, 1896." President Woodrow Wilson once dictated to his secretary in the guest suite. In 1936, just before it was razed, the building became the Democratic campaign headquarters, flying banners and a huge portrait of President Franklin Roosevelt from the balcony. The club on this site had replaced the nineteenth-century residence and detached medical office of Dr. C. J. Fox, whose home was the first in the city to be quite wondrously lit by gaslight.*

Excelsior Club. *Begun in 1944, the leading private black social club in the Southeast was the Excelsior, which stands at 921 Beatties Ford Road about one-half mile north of Johnson C. Smith University. The club is unrivaled as an Art Moderne landmark and has been an important symbol of status for upper- and middle-class black professionals since World War II. It opened with a small bar and seating for seventy-five; applicants were carefully screened for membership among Charlotte's civic and political leaders. Members gathered in the main dining room and conference room, and the entertainment hall invited them to a small stage where Nat "King" Cole and others performed. Built in 1910, the club building's physical core is a basic square house. It was extensively remodeled in 1952 with glass blocks, horizontal trim, and smooth surfaces in the Art Moderne style. The club was the dream and creation of owner Jimmie McKee. He pushed WGIV's radio station owner to broadcast live from the club and promoted radio performances by black talent. Emcee "Genial Gene" Potts entertained black radio listeners live from the club, which became a Charlotte-Mecklenburg Historic Landmark in 1986. (Courtesy Lew Powell)*

Masonic Temple, Charlotte, N. C.—15

Masonic Temple. *In 1914, Masons were rightfully proud of their new building designed by C. C. Hook and W. G. Rogers. At 329 South Tryon Street, it gave strong architectural character to the site on which earlier had been the home of Lewis Sanders. Two huge stone columns with lotus bud–cluster capitals flanked the temple's entrance. Each column held a stone globe, one incised to show the terrestrial sphere with continents, the other a celestial sphere. An exceptional example of Egyptian Revival style, the temple was demolished in 1987 and the remarkable columns purchased, moved, and reused to accompany new sculptures, "Civitas," at the formal gateway to the neighboring city of Rock Hill, South Carolina. The temple was designated a Charlotte-Mecklenburg Historic Landmark in 1980.*

Y. W. C. A. BUILDING, CHARLOTTE, N. C.

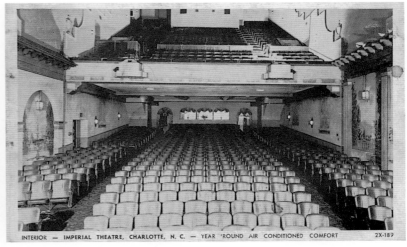

INTERIOR — IMPERIAL THEATRE, CHARLOTTE, N. C. — YEAR 'ROUND AIR CONDITIONED COMFORT   2X-189

Y. W. C. A. Building. *Around 1900, as typewriters, calculators, and business machines came into use creating clerical office tasks, young women from the country and small towns around Charlotte arrived seeking jobs. They had difficulty finding rooms to rent in respectable places. The Woman's Club efforts led to the 1902 establishment of a chapter of the Young Women's Christian Association for comfortable lodging, good meals, and a personal guide to high religious and moral standards. At first, they housed sixteen women in rented space on West Fifth Street, and later thirty-five women in a former hospital building on North Church Street behind the Selwyn Hotel. Then in 1912, the goal of $63,000 was met for this brick, three-story building with a dormitory, dining room, and gym, designed by Hook and Rogers, which opened in April 1914 at 418 East Trade Street. The campaign used the motto "Watch Charlotte Grow," adopted in 1905 by the Greater Charlotte Club (forerunner of the Charlotte Chamber). In 1922, C. C. Hook designed a swimming pool where thousands of Charlotte children learned to swim. The Y operated Camp Latta outside the city (donated by E. D. Latta), pioneered in interracial work, and owned cottages at two cotton mills for female millworkers' organized education and recreational activities. The building was demolished except for the pool in 1969 and replaced with a new YWCA on its site in 1970. This building was razed in the late 1980s.*

Imperial Theater. *Built about 1920 in the era of silent movies, the Imperial Theater at 124 South Tryon Street offered Charlotte some of its first "talkies." Until its close in 1964, it was a leading showplace of top Hollywood motion picture attractions. Fire damage prompted major remodeling in 1935, creating a romantic interior of Moorish temple design with arches, fancy drapes, carpets, and ornamental plasterwork. Stars and constellations were wondrously projected onto the ceiling. Its narrow entrance wedged between the Bank of Charlotte and Tate-Brown Co. did not deter moviegoers. The Imperial was one of four or five profitable theaters within two blocks of the Square before suburban theaters opened. In the 1930s, Henderson School of Dance met upstairs and students performed Saturday morning stage shows. The recessed balcony's far reaches were favorite nooks for dating couples. Theater manager Neil McGill sent this 1939 postcard as an ad to Mrs. Catherine Crenshaw with the handwritten note that the movie "'Four Girls in White' is made for you . . . starts Friday at the Imperial." The Imperial competed with the grand 1927 Carolina Theater on North Tryon Street, but the Carolina was larger, more dramatic, and elaborate both inside and out. The Imperial is no longer standing, but major parts of the Carolina Theater remain.*

1814 Y. M. C. A. Building, Charlotte, N. C. W. Rowland, Pub.

Y.M.C.A. Building. *When George B. Hanna came to Charlotte from the North as assayer to the U.S. Mint, he resurrected earlier Charlotte efforts (1868–71) to form an affiliate of the Young Men's Christian Association, which had begun in England. Reorganizing in 1874, the group at first rented Wadsworth Hall above Wadsworth's Stables on North Tryon Street for a meeting room and lecture courses. They soon rented other buildings and raised funds at a revival meeting and campaign for the first YMCA building in the Carolinas, pictured here at 206 South Tryon Street. The building, completed in 1888 for $40,000, was a handsome, three-story brownstone with arched Romanesque windows, a turret and tower, and two street-level shops for rental. The interior had frescoed walls, dormitory rooms, a gym, tennis and basketball courts, a reading room with 2,500 volumes, and an auditorium seating 750 for lectures and entertainments. The Y conducted a night school and a boarding-house information bureau. This building was sold in 1905 and a nearby site was purchased for a new five-story Y. When the building came down to be replaced by the new American Trust Building, forerunner of Bank of America, the newspaper reported in 1909: "'It really seems a pity,' said an onlooker, 'to tear down a building altogether so presentable as the old YMCA.' 'On the contrary,' said a progressive citizen, 'that's the best sign I've seen of Charlotte's advancement.'"*

Y. M. C. A. and Latta Arcade, Charlotte, N. C.

Y.M.C.A. and Latta Arcade. *The architectural firm of Hook and Rogers designed this 1908 building (left) for the Young Men's Christian Association with additions in 1915, 1916, and 1921 in the 300 block of South Tryon Street at Second Street. Built by J. A. Jones Construction Co. for $145,000 including the lot, the roof garden and dormitory rooms for male boarders impressed Charlotteans: carpeted floors, lavatories, commodious closets, and chiffoniers. A big to-do was made at the opening in 1908, when twenty members of the boys' department hauled a "great galvanized iron flag-staff" to the roof with long ropes where it was ready for the afternoon unfurling of a huge American flag. In 1924 the Y had 1,600 members, and in 1939 it was renovated acquiring a new pool and enlarged health club. By 1950, it could house 166 boarders in its three floors of rooms. It was demolished in 1960.*

Next door is the two-story Latta Arcade (right) at 320 South Tryon Street. It is a treasure of the National Register of Historic Places and became a Charlotte-Mecklenburg Historic Landmark in 1978. Opening in 1915, this arcade is one of Charlotte's most important buildings because it has maintained a very functional and sophisticated original design which features a beautiful, elaborate staircase, and it originally housed the offices of one of Charlotte's most important historic figures, E. D. Latta. Latta conceived and developed Dilworth, Charlotte's first New South neighborhood which opened in 1891. He owned the first electric trolley line and lured Charlotteans out to his park pavilion and homesites to "buy a home with the rent money," a novel idea at the time. His office for the important 4C's Company was at the top of the marble stairs leading from the arcade.

Designed by architect William H. Peeps, the Beaux Arts–style commercial arcade is a pedestrian passage linking two parallel streets. At the entrance, Peeps's design features a gable roof, green Spanish tiles, and decorative modillions. A gigantic skylight not only brightens the pedestrian thoroughfare but once aided cotton brokers on the second floor with natural light to grade the piles of cotton. A 1920s layout map shows eighteen street-level offices and several stores in the covered arcade. Spanning the front half of the block, the arcade then extends to an open rear court, named Brevard Court after Dr. R. L. Brevard, who owned the site. The uncovered court held twenty-three commercial spaces which in 1924 were deemed "a kind of local cotton exchange, offices largely inhabited by cotton agencies." A modern facade was added in the 1950s, and in 1989, architects Meyer and Greeson altered it to conform to Peeps's original design.

Trust Building and YMCA. *The richly ornamented pediment of the Trust Building* (left), *which opened in 1902, intentionally stood out in any view of South Tryon Street. As the second office building in the uptown district of Charlotte, its owners wanted it to be the handsomest. It had elevators and two broad flights of stairs leading to offices and the well-known Academy of Music. The Academy was Charlotte's second "opera house," a term common in the era for a theater with a stage and dressing rooms. The Academy had 1,350 seats on several levels for viewing touring vaudeville shows, drama, comedies, concert singers, magicians, or operas, such as Bizet's* Carmen, *which was performed in 1902. Designed by Hook and Rogers at 210–212 South Tryon Street, the Trust Building also housed offices of the American Trust Co., Catawba and Southern Power Companies, Stuart Cramer's office, and realty companies. Nicholas Ittner of Atlanta was the contractor. A disastrous late-night fire in 1922 destroyed the beloved theater and building. The Johnston Building was built on the site in 1924.*

Charlotte, N.C. Trust Building and Y. M. C. A.

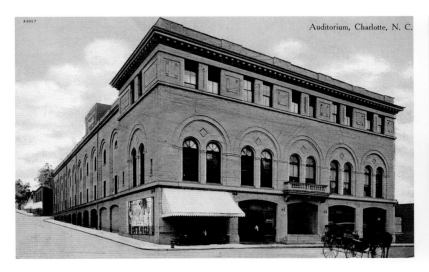

Auditorium, Charlotte, N. C.

Fair Grounds, Playtime, Charlotte, N. C.

Auditorium. *This multi-use Civic Auditorium built at the northwest corner of College and East Fifth Streets was far more handsome outside than in. The three-story interior was a yawning network of steel beams across the lofty ceiling. The concrete floor and entire building were advertised as fireproof, since the earlier auditorium burned after only four years' use. Designed by architect L. L. Hunter, it seated 4,500 people, although plans had projected 5,000 seats on the main floor, balcony, and gallery levels. Seats evidently were movable on the main floor, to accommodate such varied events as band concerts by John Philip Sousa, lectures by Will Rogers and William Jennings Bryan, and arias by tenor Enrico Caruso. It then alternated as a skating rink and dance floor with live bands. The facility opened in 1908 for the Democratic State Convention. An advertisement in 1909 heralded a basketball game with all players on skates. Street-front and interior shops were at ground level, with two rooms for military meetings. Wide stairs led to open auditorium space on both the second and third floors. The building was dismantled in 1932 and rebuilt on Tuckaseegee Road as Garr Tabernacle.*

Fair Grounds. *The Fairgrounds in Dilworth was a leased expanse of forty acres along the south side of East Boulevard, which included a ballpark and land beyond. Its opening in September 1902 drew 5,000 spectators for horse races, exhibitions, and events on the midway. E. D. Latta's 4C's Company completed a new section of the trolley line just in time to take Charlotteans to the newly opened recreation area. The race track stood in the vicinity of Park Road and Dilworth Road West. The fairgrounds and ballpark 1½ miles from uptown made Latta Park the center of Charlotte sports from 1902 until 1911. At the race track, fair officials charged admission to view an early airplane flight in Charlotte. The plane flew only 100 feet along the oval track, and winds caused it to wreck, greatly adding to the spectacle. When the lease expired in 1911, Latta contracted the noted Olmsted Brothers of Massachusetts, America's most prestigious landscape firm, to develop the former ballpark and fairgrounds land and adjacent parcels for new homes.*

Base Ball Park, Playtime, Charlotte, N. C.

Base Ball Park (top); **Hornets 1909** (bottom). *Charlotteans were thrilled by the permanent baseball park built in 1892 in Latta Park by the company that developed Dilworth. It had grandstand seating for 2,500 spectators. Charlotte's professional club vied for the pennant in the South Atlantic League. Charlotte's colored baseball club played teams from Athens and Atlanta, Georgia. In 1892, admission to the ball ground in Latta Park was a quarter for men and fifteen cents for ladies and children. In 1902, Charlotte's baseball team became a member of the Carolina League, but it folded before the close of the season. Eddie Ashenback was manager. One newspaper described a 1905 game between the Charlotte "immovables" and the Davidson "irresistibles," saying, "Dr. Alexander, manager for Charlotte, deserved particular mention for scattering lime along the tracks. He did this beautifully." The baseball park pictured here was in use around 1908.*

Another baseball team to come to Charlotte, in 1908, were the Hornets, managed by Lave Cross. A year later the Hornets were pictured on this postcard. C. F. Humphrey (top, second from right) was their leading hitter. Within three years the Hornets were playing in a new park, Wearn field and grandstand, which was built on Mint Street in 1911–12 and designed by Louis Asbury Sr. It replaced the Latta baseball park when its ten-year lease expired. Park Road got its name from the Latta Park sports field. The Hornets shared Wearn Field with at least one northern team during a preseason, when the Brooklyn Dodgers held their spring training in Charlotte. (Courtesy Sarah Manning Pope Collection)

CH..3.   CHARLOTTE SPEEDWAY, CHARLOTTE, N. C.   107432

Charlotte Speedway, Charlotte, N. C.—44
5000 Autos parked in the infield.

Charlotte Speedway. *In 1924, a persuasive promoter with an English accent sold several Charlotte leaders on the idea that a Charlotte speedway would bring the city fame and money. It took some tall convincing, but Jack Prince, a well-known track architect, was up to the job. Investors put up $300,000 to build a 1.25-mile plank track of green pine and cypress. In forty days, it was completed, seating 24,000 fans.*

Even the catapulting death of one of the racers in practice did not deter the opening in October 1924. Approximately 35,000 fans came, traveling the nine miles from Charlotte mostly by free trains to the 282-acre site just north of Pineville. Tobacco tycoon James B. Duke sat in the stands watching. Promoters cleared $25,000 and arranged another race, which led to later racing events, larger speedways, and, yes, NASCAR! One official boasted in 1924, "A million dollars would not buy the publicity that has come to Charlotte as a result of the race." The Great Depression and serious weather damage caused its closing.

Charlotte Polo Club. *A competitive network of Carolina polo teams at Pinehurst, Winston-Salem, and Camden persuaded Charlotte polo enthusiasts to organize a team in the 1920s. Many members lived in Myers Park, where they had horses and stables adjacent to their homes. Members rode their horses on Sunday afternoons at first to a field at the corner of Selwyn Avenue and Queens Road West, which was donated for polo practice by the Stephens Co. It was also used as an informal airfield; about two planes landed there a day. The Polo Club subsequently moved to the site pictured on the edge of Myers Park along Sugar Creek bottomland, where they had a stableman, stables with drain tiles, a barn, and polo grounds in front. In the late 1940s, the polo grounds became a part of Freedom Park.*

Vance Park. *On an October afternoon in 1905, President Theodore Roosevelt spoke from the bandstand in this park at Fourth and Mint Streets during an hour-long whistlestop visit. The small park was federal property, right behind the large, brick post office building at Mint and Trade Streets and the Charlotte U.S. Mint. A wrought-iron fence enclosed the park, where curious Charlotteans crowded inside and beyond the fence. Roosevelt's rousing eulogy of Confederate general Stonewall Jackson led him to pick up and kiss Jackson's small granddaughter who stood beside him. The crowd roared approval. The shady park with benches and a fountain was named for Governor Zebulon Baird Vance. The raised bandstand (center) was often the site of temperance speeches. Charlotte's Park and Tree Commission gave Mr. Scholtz, a florist, permission to build a florist shop and greenhouse on the edge of Vance Park, which he did, but the paint was barely dry before the federal government decided to expand the post office, eliminating Mr. Scholtz's popular flowers. Earlier the park was known as Mint Park.*

Latta Park. *This peaceful, country scene with flowers and paths for strolling couples was only one feature of popular Latta Park, created in the streetcar neighborhood of Dilworth beginning in the 1890s. Visitors enjoyed boating excursions on the quarter-mile length of Lake Forsythe, the 10,000-square-foot greenhouse, a summer stock theater for concerts and performances, and a dramatic towered pavilion whose entertainments included a ten-pin alley (bowling), and a skating rink with music and dancing. The pavilion was designed by Swedish-born architect Gottfrid L. Norrman of Atlanta, then known in the South as an "architect of beautiful designs." Annie Oakley performed here in a massive tent in 1901 as part of Buffalo Bill Cody's "Wild West Show."*

Latta was a privately owned ninety-acre park open to the public, the first for Charlotte at a time when recreational parks were a new idea. Developer E. D. Latta hoped visitors to the park in Dilworth would be so impressed they would buy a lot on the installment plan in this "vicinity of picturesque places." The lake was later drained which created a much smaller Latta Park.

Electric Car Line Depot "Lakewood," Charlotte, N. C.
The Industrial Centre of the New South.

The Roller Coaster at "Lakewood" Charlotte, N. C.
The Industrial Centre of the New South

A PICTURESQUE VIEW IN LAKEWOOD PARK, CHARLOTTE, N. C.

Lakewood. *The dreariest job could be endured with the promise of frolic at Lakewood, with its dancing pavilion featuring Santini's Italian band (two concerts daily), swingsets, forty-three rowboats, swimming, a roller coaster, a merry-go-round, and a zoo. Just west of Tuckaseegee Road, all of these attractions were easily accessible in the early 1900s by rail from Charlotte. Five nearby streets were named for this park, including Lakeview Street and Parkway Avenue. Daring circus feats drew great crowds. Jack Taylor, "The Human Torch," was one. Ablaze, he descended sixty feet in a chute into the lake, "tempting Providence." Michigan balloonist H. C. Brown landed by mistake in the lake during a 1911 performance and drowned. Following its grand opening on July 9, 1910, Lakewood was advertised as a "mecca for excursions" and "the most complete and cleanest amusement resort between Washington and Atlanta." Floods washed out the dam in April 1936, and the park was abandoned. The parents of world-famous evangelist and Charlotte native Billy Graham met at a picnic at Lakewood Park.*

A PAVILION AT LAKEWOOD PARK, CHARLOTTE, N. C.

TWO OF THE PETS AT LAKEWOOD PARK, CHARLOTTE, N. C.

BABY MAY

DAUGHTER OF RUTH AND BOAZ

First Ostrich hatched in North Carolina
Lakewood Park, Charlotte, N. C.
August 14, 1915.

Charlotte, N. C., The Industrial Center of the New South,
Special North Carolina Barbecue.

Barbecue. *The faint postcard inscription across the tablecloth's skirt reads "Charlotte, Center of the Industrial South, Special North Carolina Barbecue." Since the men in this photo are sporting political buttons, this might be a pre-election gathering at Latta Park (note streetcar conductor, far right). The fellows look like city folk who came out to eat barbecue, shake hands, and gather votes (a Mecklenburg tradition).*

4. Governmental Business *Courthouses, City Halls, Public Buildings*

THE FIRST COURT IN MECKLENBURG COUNTY, FEBRUARY 26, 1763, CHARLOTTE, N. C.   123063

13408—Old Mecklenburg County Court House, Charlotte. N. C.

Site of the First Court. *Words on the tall granite boulder by the sidewalk in the 1900 block, Randolph Road, declare where county court was first held. "Site of the First Court Held in Mecklenburg County, February 26, 1763, Home of Thomas Spratt, First Person to Cross the Yadkin River with Wheels. Here Was Born His Daughter Anne Spratt, First White Child Born Between Catawba & Yadkin Rivers." Two young Charlotte girls, Alice Alexander (right) and Sarah Belk (left), stand beside the marker erected in 1926. Spratt settled on this high knoll just east of what would become the village of Charlottetown.*

The county's first courthouse (1766–1810) was a rustic log building on six or eight ten-foot pillars with an outside stair and open space beneath for a street-level market. Town leaders enclosed this "exchange" in 1779 to keep out wandering hogs, sheep, and horses. The log structure was covered in 1783. It sat in the center of intersecting roads, the Catawba Trading Path (later Tryon Street) and a trading route of pioneer settlers (later Trade Street). The area of the crossroads and the courthouse became known as Courthouse Square and later Independence Square. Close by was a town common or open space.

The second courthouse stood in the same location (1810–45) and was a fancier, two-story brick structure with a hipped roof and cupola.

Third Courthouse, northeast corner West Trade and Church Streets *(1845–97). Four covered brick columns, each about three feet in diameter, attempted a more imposing look for the backcountry town. First-floor offices and the second-story courtroom with jury rooms were warmed by fireplaces. Courtroom furnishings included a bench, bar, clerks' table, and jury seats. Two wooden columns supported the courtroom gallery above, and the crowd was often rowdy and messy, with watermelon eaters and riffraff. In 1891, the courthouse janitor says, "86 melons were dissected in the jury room today. The leak in the jury room has not yet been stopped, either, and every time a shower comes up, the jury has to scatter for shelter." In back of the building was a standpipe for water storage built in 1881, a fire bell in a tall belfry, and space for Negro hirings and auctions from carts and wagons. After demolition in 1905, leftover bricks were reused for foundations of what would become the Selwyn Hotel on the same site.*

G 12127 Court House, Charlotte, N C   Copyright 1905 by the Rotograph Co.

C-31:—MECKLENBURG COUNTY COURT HOUSE, CHARLOTTE, N. C.

Fourth Courthouse, 301 South Tryon Street *(1896–1928). With a large, leafy, open plaza from the portico steps to South Tryon Street, this "Victorian version of a European capitol building" which some termed "pretentious" was designed by Charlotte architect Frank P. Milburn. More than twenty U.S. architects submitted plans. The buff brick and stone building with marble floors held two second-story courtrooms with stairways and an open portico surmounted by a large dome, with a balcony facing the plaza. County offices on the first and basement floors were declared "outmoded and overcrowded in less than 30 years." Problems also with theft were reported, particularly from an upstairs room where officials stored confiscated spirits, leading to the practice of pouring the whisky down the gutter. Just to the south of the plaza stood the Lawyers' Building.*

Fifth Courthouse, 700 East Trade Street *(1928–78). Designed by Charlotte architect Louis Asbury Sr., this imposing, classical revival facility held an interior court garage with a secret tunnel for prisoners and a special jail elevator to cells on the fourth floor. The criminal court occupied the second floor and at the opposite end was the civil court with a balcony seating for "colored folks attending court and is made private for them by a spiral stairway reaching to a special entrance on the ground floor." One judge found the Roman colonnade reminiscent of historical Roman law and Empire Palladian window treatments echoing Napoleonic Code of Laws. Great controversy arose when the location of this building was proposed, moving it blocks away from Tryon Street which folks felt was the heart of the community. One rural justice of the peace said "country people" would never find a courthouse built on Trade Street and therefore couldn't pay their taxes. A sixth courthouse was dedicated in 1978 at 800 East Fourth Street with the Fifth Courthouse building remaining in use.*

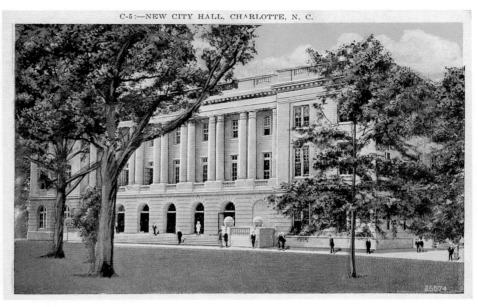

City Hall. *Since the 1880s, Charlotte's City Hall (government center) successively grew grander, reflecting civic pride and local ambition. This 1925 City Hall at 600 East Trade Street removed civic offices from North Tryon Street to a site east of the Square, utilizing a full city block with space for parklike surroundings and an elegant view from all sides. The neoclassical design by C. C. Hook handsomely provided mayoral and city manager offices and city departments above a grand lobby of Tennessee marble with wide marble staircases. The three-story building of Indiana limestone engaged the eye with its arched entrances and windows, colonnaded facade, and balustrade. Later, small auxiliary buildings of complementary design for fire, police, and welfare departments were removed when the governmental plaza was redesigned and the 1989 Charlotte-Mecklenburg Government Center at 600 East Fourth Street, designed by Philip Shive, was built. At the end of the twentieth century, this building remains as civic offices with parklike surroundings and war memorials of various eras placed on the grounds. It became a Charlotte-Mecklenburg Historic Landmark in 1980.*

CHARLOTTE, N.C. City Hall.

City Hall *(1891–1924). Charlotte was quite proud of this brownstone city hall, designed by Gottfrid L. Norrman of Atlanta. The tall tower with its signature dragon weathervane was visible all over town and contained a city clock with a face on each of the four sides and a deep bell which boomed out the hour. The castle-like building and its tower dominated the southeast corner of North Tryon and Fifth Streets, the site where the North Carolina Blumenthal Performing Arts Center opened in 1992.*

View showing Post Office, Assay Office and Shipp Monument, Charlotte, N.C.

U.S. Post Office. *When the* Charlotte News *reported the construction in August 1890 of this new federal post office building at 401 West Trade Street, it praised the "monument to the first Democratic administration in 26 years past, for it was secured under the Cleveland administration, plans drawn by William Freret, Democrat supervising architect." The building for which Congress appropriated $92,500 was completed in 1891, not 1881 as is often reported. The exterior was brick with terra cotta and* white stone trim accented by an eighty-four-foot tower which gave a "fine view of the mountain ranges." Inside were marble columns, marble and tile floors, polished oak woodwork, and corridors with blue marble baseboards. The entire first floor was used as a post office with 576 postal boxes of beveled French glass. Upstairs, the U.S. courtroom shared the second floor with court and revenue offices. It was demolished in 1915 for replacement by a larger post office and courthouse on the same corner.*

UNITED STATES POST OFFICE AND COURT HOUSE, CHARLOTTE, N. C.

U.S. Post Office and Courthouse. *Charlotte's growth quickly outdated the handsome brick 1891 federal post office at 401 West Trade Street, so it was razed for replacement by this new Renaissance Revival, limestone structure on the same site, completed in 1918. Its "completion" was short-lived however. A much-needed expansion created many Depression-era jobs when the 1918 building was tripled in size with a design by Charlotte architect C. C. Hook. The central neoclassical entrance and new west wing balanced the existing east wing and completed the formidable governmental presence in 1934. To make room for this expansion, the original U.S. Mint building on this site was dismantled and later rebuilt.*

Jonas Building. *Inside this 1934 structure is the majestic courtroom and impressive marble wainscoting, intricate ceilings, and hardware. The postal service moved to other quarters in the 1970s. In 1984, this building was dedicated as the Charles Raper Jonas Building named for the Republican Congressman elected to five consecutive terms beginning in 1952. It is on the National Register of Historic Places.*

Mint Museum of Art, Charlotte, N. C.

7A-H2892

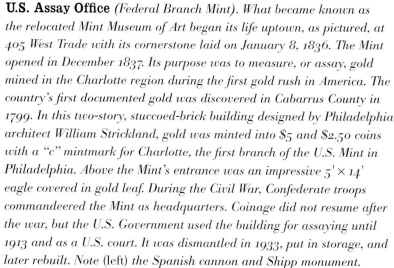

Charlotte, N. C. Shipp Monument and U. S. Assay Office

U.S. Assay Office *(Federal Branch Mint). What became known as the relocated Mint Museum of Art began its life uptown, as pictured, at 405 West Trade with its cornerstone laid on January 8, 1836. The Mint opened in December 1837. Its purpose was to measure, or assay, gold mined in the Charlotte region during the first gold rush in America. The country's first documented gold was discovered in Cabarrus County in 1799. In this two-story, stuccoed-brick building designed by Philadelphia architect William Strickland, gold was minted into $5 and $2.50 coins with a "c" mintmark for Charlotte, the first branch of the U.S. Mint in Philadelphia. Above the Mint's entrance was an impressive 5' × 14' eagle covered in gold leaf. During the Civil War, Confederate troops commandeered the Mint as headquarters. Coinage did not resume after the war, but the U.S. Government used the building for assaying until 1913 and as a U.S. court. It was dismantled in 1933, put in storage, and later rebuilt. Note (left) the Spanish cannon and Shipp monument.*

Mint Museum of Art. *Martin Evans Boyer Jr., a Charlotte architect, donated his services in the rebuilding of the Mint as the Mint Museum of Art. It opened in 1936. The museum faced Hempstead Place in what was then the new neighborhood of Eastover, designed in 1927. The location had previously been bottomland of a large dairy farm with woodland and pastures along Briar Creek extending toward Providence Road. In the 1920s, children who lived along Hermitage Court near the earlier neighborhood of Myers Park held their own "Saturday School" in a playhouse, and after lessons teaching each other the French or math they'd learned that week, they took an afternoon picnic, walking "east over the hill" down toward Briar Creek. When E. C. Griffith bought the farm for his new development, he adopted the name Eastover. In 1985, the Mint expanded, kept the historic face intact, but reversed its main entrance to a lofty modern facade and fountain fronting on 2730 Randolph Road. The Mint is the oldest art museum in North Carolina and contains ceramics, paintings, and a gold exhibit. It became a Charlotte-Mecklenburg Historic Landmark in 1976.*

Charlotte, N. C. Stand Pipe. Second largest of its kind in the United States.

They called it "The Standpipe," *a local marvel built in 1905 to supply water to the townspeople. At the corner of North Graham and West Fifth Streets, the steel-plate structure replaced an earlier one behind the third County Courthouse. H. E. Boardman of New York was the architect and consulting engineer of the thirty-foot diameter and 135-foot-high watertower, which was covered "so that nothing could get in it." It could hold 715,000 gallons of water and was second only to a taller standpipe in Houston, Texas.*

The handsome home pictured here was the residence (1890s to about 1911) of one of Charlotte's most important men, Samuel Wittkowsky. He was a Prussian immigrant who came to this area in 1855, poor and friendless. He worked his way to ownership of a very prosperous mercantile business and extensive real estate holdings. Known widely as the "building and loan king of North Carolina," he was called "the most useful citizen of Charlotte."

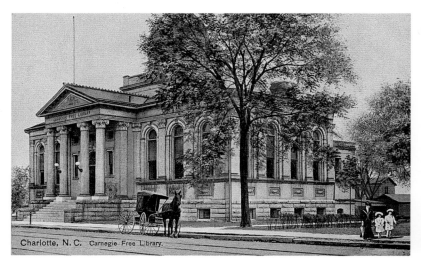

Charlotte, N. C. Carnegie Free Library.

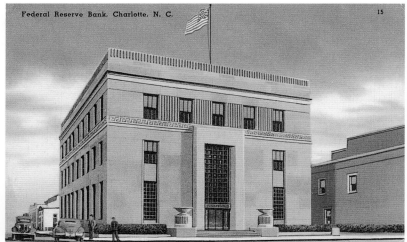

Federal Reserve Bank. Charlotte. N. C.   15

Carnegie Library. *When the N.C. General Assembly incorporated the Charlotte Literary and Library Association in 1891, the library operated upstairs in a South Tryon Street bookstore, much like a "literary club where visitors come in for a book and stay to talk." Alderman Thomas S. Franklin Sr. secured a $25,000 grant from steel magnate Andrew Carnegie for construction of a library. Carnegie agreed, provided the city furnish an agreeable site and support the library with no less than $2,500 annually. Architects Oliver D. Wheeler and J. M. McMichael drew plans for a classical four-columned central portico and a domed cupola at 310 North Tryon Street. It opened in July 1903. With a 1915 addition funded by Carnegie, the library gained a children's area and auditorium for a community "town hall." The library was razed in 1954 and a new library was built in 1956 on the same site, with major renovation and expansion in 1989. The library was not a Victorian-era idea. Early settlers Hezekiah Alexander, Waightstill Avery, Adam Alexander, and others gave books to the Mecklenburg Library, established in 1771. The library was believed to have been located at Queen's College for boys, established the same year. The college was the first one chartered in North Carolina.*

Federal Reserve Bank Building. *Designed by Baltimore architects Taylor and Fisher, this Charlotte Branch of the Federal Reserve of Richmond at 401 South Tryon Street was a clear monument to the city's commercial success when it opened in 1942. The Federal Reserve had begun its Charlotte presence in 1927. That event, more than any other, signaled the importance of the city as a New South center of industrialism, keyed to finance and cotton textile manufacturing growth since the 1880s. From this facility, the Federal Reserve served the industrial Piedmont region of the Carolinas. The three-story building of North Carolina granite topped with Indiana limestone had Tennessee marble floors and bronze entry grillwork. It blended Art Moderne, Art Deco, and neoclassical styles. In 1950s, an addition doubled the building's size. In 1988, the bank moved to a new building at 530 East Trade Street. The building on the postcard and adjacent buildings were demolished in 1997 by First Union Corporation for a thirty-story office and retail tower. The Charlotte Observer saw palpable irony in this, since "The Federal Reserve's decision to open a Charlotte branch sparked the city's growth as a banking center, leading to such giants as NationsBank [now Bank of America] and First Union."*

Copyright 1905 by the Rotograph Co.

G 12128 City Hall, Charlotte, N C.

Charlotte Hotel. *In this postcard view from 1905 stood the frame, two-story Charlotte Hotel at 30 North Tryon Street, next to the statuesque City Hall building. Its varied history, dating back at least to 1825, brought in a new name and owner every few years, along with new customers of its food, lodging, and entertainment. As early as July 1825, a hospitable establishment stood here known as Dr. Samuel Henderson's Tavern. In 1826, Robert I. Dinkins promoted his House of Entertainment, offering a bar, stables, food, and careful servants. By 1830, the name Charlotte Hotel was in use under the ownership of Joshua D. Boyd, whose ad declared, "The beds and bedding are inferior to none." In 1856, the hotel held the stagecoach office for passengers traveling west to Asheville or south to Camden, South Carolina. Yet another owner, Major Jennings Kerr, renamed it Carolina Inn, and he never failed to serve chicken pie in a yellow Queensware dish. Again the name Charlotte Hotel was placed over the door, and by 1892, a notice boasted new electric fans in the dining room. J. W. Brown ran the hotel from the early 1900s until 1917. Finally called the Evermore Hotel, it defied its ambitious name and burned. Later, Efird's Department Store occupied the site.*

CHARLOTTE, N. C.   Central Hotel.
4003

Central Hotel. *In advertisements, this hotel claimed it "Pleases All People All The Time," providing "Good Rooms, Good Beds, Good Table, Electric Fans in Dining Room." Through a series of different names and owners, the Central operated on its highly popular southeast corner of Trade and Tryon Streets from 1840 to the 1930s. It was first called a tavern, then the Sadler's Hotel in 1846, and later the Mansion House. It was rebuilt in 1853–54 with the city's most elegant bar and a high-ceilinged dining room. In early days a bowl and pitcher supplied bath water to rooms, although a tin tub of hot water was brought upon request. Exotic guests came through, such as bearded Count Tyrzi, of Russian royalty, who stopped here by train in 1875 traveling from Florida to New York with servants and twenty-five Saratoga trunks. The elaborate Thanksgiving menu in 1889 offered quail, crabs, and opossum with vegetables. A 1909 menu included Consommé en Tasse, Ham with Champagne Sauce, Pear Pie or Camembert Cheese served with Derita Water. After dinner, music was provided by Richardson's orchestra. In 1938, a local gentleman watered his horse at the Central Hotel bar from "a punch bowl while he sat in the saddle and drank his spirits." The four-story hotel had no elevator but was considered the finest hotel between Richmond and Atlanta. On the main floor it had ornate gaslit chandeliers, shining brass cuspidors, and elaborate wallpaper designs above wainscoting. A special ladies' entrance sheltered the fair sex from the indiscretion of being seen entering the main hotel. Three of Charlotte's most famous men boarded here until they married: William Henry Belk, Edward Dilworth Latta, and newspaper editor Joseph P. Caldwell. In 1931, the Central's 125 rooms became the Albert Hotel; it was later razed and replaced by the S. H. Kress and Co., a large five-and-dime store (1942–73), and subsequently by the Bank of America Plaza.*

Hotel BUFORD, Charlotte, N. C. C. E. Hooper & Co., Proprietors

Buford Hotel. *Because the Buford was, as advertised, "Headquarters of Cotton Mill Men" and the "Traveling Men's Home," these "drummers" between 1885 and 1915 filled Charlotte's second most important hotel. Often sitting in rustic chairs and benches out front at 139 South Tryon Street (northeast corner at Fourth Street), the men caused local ladies to avoid the corner and the indelicate remarks they might attract. Thomas Edison and Alexander Graham Bell stayed here on visits to Charlotte. In 1890, the Buford Hotel was enlarged to include the city's first elevator and a fourth-floor roof-garden dining room. Named for Colonel A. S. Buford, president of the Richmond and Danville Railroad, the Buford Company was steered by prominent Charlotte textile men Horace Johnston and R. M. Miller Jr. Guests enjoyed the Buford Bar, Brussels carpets, oak furniture, and "the very best beds" at $2–3 a day.*

But the Buford was more than a hotel. Built for offices in 1870, it housed at street level two banks that grew into financial-service giants. The Commercial National Bank was organized here in 1874 and was later moved across the street to become a cornerstone of the Bank of America empire. Union National Bank was organized here in 1908 and flourished until after World War II, when it was moved farther south on Tryon Street and grew into the sprawling First Union Corporation. Early in the building's life, it also housed the U.S. Post Office and, on the second floor, the U.S. District Court. The building also housed the Charlotte City Club, whose members dined there from 1946 to the 1960s. The building had been converted to hotel uses in 1885, and toward the end of its life it returned to that role and was known as the Piedmont Hotel. The singular corner design and tiny tower make the three-story hotel with its annex easy to spot in streetscapes. It was demolished to make room for the Home Federal Savings and Loan building. First Charter Corporation acquired Home Federal in 1998.

CHARLOTTE, N. C.   Selwyn Hotel

E. 9302

Charlotte, N.C.
The Industrial Centre of the New South

DINING ROOM

Three interior views of the Selwyn Hotel The most luxurious American Plan Hotel in the South Harvey & Wood, Mgrs.

LOBBY.   GROUND FLOOR PARLOR.

Selwyn Hotel. *The opening of this ambitious six-story hotel in 1907 marks a bold bid to attract convention business and "hifalutin"' vacation travelers, bringing "a new class of patronage to the city." The Highland Hotels Co. chose Atlanta architect W. F. Denny for the posh hotel, hoping to lure train travelers between Atlanta and New York or Pinehurst and Asheville to "break their journey" with a stopover in Charlotte. The immense hotel at the northeast corner of West Trade and North Church Streets was named for Lord Selwyn, the English owner of the lands purchased for the early town of Charlotte. Bricks from the old "third Courthouse" were cleared to prepare the site for a new emblem of the modern era, which would provide for both Charlotteans and travelers the best dining room in town as well as banquet rooms and a convention hall.*

Promotions boasted of the hotel's lower-level barber shop, pool room, ice plant and Turkish bath, the telegraph office, long-distance phone booths, a newsstand, and electric lights for the 75 rooms with baths, and a total of 150 rooms. "Every room [was] an outside room with telephones and running water." Rooms with private baths were $2–3 daily, or $5 for the bridal chamber with its emerald view, tendrils and blooms on wallpaper, and carpet touted as "the floral beauty of eden." The Poppy Room was a "shrine to the divinity of sleep." Famous guests were opera singer Enrico Caruso, boxing champion Jack Dempsey, and visiting U.S. presidents, who expected these amenities. Another major asset was its modern construction to make the Selwyn the "first fireproof hotel in North Carolina." Its large lobby and reception rooms had Venetian mosaic with marble wainscoting and decorative ceilings. The Selwyn Hotel was remodeled in 1948 with air conditioning and showers, but it closed in 1964 and later became the site of the Charlotte Marriott Center.

Stonewall Hotel and Annex, Charlotte, North Carolina

Southern Railway Passenger Station

WALTON HOTEL — 5TH AND COLLEGE STREET. CHARLOTTE. NORTH CAROLINA.

JOHN C. BATTEN. PROP. CENTRALLY LOCATED. PHONE 5107

Stonewall Hotel and Travelers Hotel (left). *Popular Washington-based architect Frank Milburn designed the Stonewall Hotel, built in 1907 at 535 West Trade Street and closed in 1958. Advertisements heralded its ace location next to the Southern Railway Station (portico visible at right) and claimed, "Every Traveling Man Travels for the Stonewall" with "123 rooms, 50 rooms with private bath, hot and cold water in all rooms." It also boasted such benefits as "A homelike hotel, where every consideration is given." The hotel's name, carved in the upper facade, was well chosen, for the structure not only sat on property that had been one of the Charlotte homesites of Mrs. Stonewall Jackson, but it also attracted nostalgic old soldiers and their families who were traveling through. In 1909, the white duck–clad waiters made the news when "all the colored waiters of the Stonewall Hotel, led by Charlie Thompson, head waiter, went on strike for the reason that they were not allowed chicken fried, stewed, and fricasseed with their meals just like the guests." Bell boys and others took the strikers' places. The Travelers Hotel (left) began advertising in 1941 and was last listed in the 1994 City Directory. Ads claimed its fortunate location at 533 West Trade Street: "Clean, Comfortable, Convenient. Reasonable Rates. Between Southern Railway and the Bus Station."*

Walton Hotel. *Plain-folk travelers and long-term tenants often chose small uptown hotels for what the Walton called "Homelike Atmosphere of Respectability at Moderate Cost." The three-story Walton Hotel with its modest entrance at 204 North College Street amicably shared its street-front space with Rogers Paint Store, which sold wallpaper and glass at the convenient corner of College and Fifth Streets. Its postcard ad tells guests that they can count on running water, which in the 1920s was not to be taken for granted. The postcard also specifies "comfort, security, steam heat and a telephone in every room and convenient parking." The Walton was last listed in the 1958 City Directory.*

Mecklenburg Hotel, Charlotte, N. C.

Mecklenburg Hotel. *The best place to eat in Charlotte around 1950 was a French restaurant at 516 West Trade Street in the Mecklenburg Hotel, built in 1914. A plaque touting the hotel read, "Good enough for everybody. Not too good for anybody." Architect Louis Asbury Sr. designed the brick five-story, 160-room hotel for the Mecklenburg Hotel Company. It sat conveniently across from the train depot on the former homesite and garden of John and Jane Wilkes, owners of the Mecklenburg Iron Works. Theirs was one of many impressive homes that had previously lined West Trade Street in the mid- to late 1800s. Rooms in the Mecklenburg Hotel were small, but the food was very good in the reign of chef Henri Montet. At Chez Montet, wrote one reporter, soft music and sweet smells drifted into the lobby. Goose liver with truffles was routine. One night, noted actor Charles Laughton savored a delectable veal dish at a corner table. Laughton toured out of his way to visit Chez Montet saying, "Word about good food gets around."*

In 1916, Knoxville publisher Curtis B. Johnson entertained Charlotte developer George Stephens and banker Word Wood at the Mecklenburg Hotel. With them Johnson negotiated his purchase of the Charlotte Observer, which he built into the Carolinas' largest daily newspaper. Wrestlers on tour liked the hotel as a convenient 1960s stopover between Atlanta and Richmond. Among the colorful performers was Gorgeous George traveling with blonde Cherie, who ceremonially sprayed perfume in his corner of the wrestling ring before each match. In 1975, deputies padlocked the run-down hotel. "It was allowed to reopen after agreeing to try to ban known prostitutes." About 1979, the hotel burned and was soon demolished.

Hotel Charlotte. *For much of its nearly fifty years, Hotel Charlotte was the city's most important hotel beginning in 1924. New York's W. L. Stoddart, noted architect of large American hotels, designed this twelve-story landmark at 237 West Trade Street, built by J. A. Jones Construction Co. For Charlotte, it was extravagant with its large, marbled lobby and mirrored ballroom. The original 254 rooms were later enlarged to 400. The front and street-side exterior contained complex symbols celebrating the city's role in the American Revolution, a sculpted liberty tree and torches, a hornets' nest, and the date 1775 among garlands, rosettes, swags, and cartouches. It exemplified the city's exuberant 1920s textile-based prosperity. Funds for hotel construction were raised from citizen subscriptions of 600 local stockholders. Famous guests included Presidents Franklin Roosevelt and Richard Nixon, boxing champion Jack Dempsey, baseball great Babe Ruth, and bandleaders Guy Lombardo and Tommy Dorsey. In 1937, RCA used three tenth-floor rooms as a recording studio for Bill and Charlie Monroe, Roy Acuff, and many other southern artists. At one period in the street-level cafe called the Tavern, there was a table for nine which locals dubbed "the city hall of Charlotte." The hotel became the Queen Charlotte Hotel in 1961, and it closed in 1973 as the White House Inn. After the hotel closed, it was placed on the National Register of Historic Places. It became a Charlotte-Mecklenburg Historic Landmark in 1984. It was imploded in 8½ seconds in 1988 to make room for the Carillon Building.*

THE HOTEL CHARLOTTE, CHARLOTTE, N. C.   89273

29 — MAYFAIR HOTEL, CHARLOTTE, N. C.

Mayfair Manor/Dunhill Hotel. *In 1929, one month after the stock market crash that preceded the Great Depression, the elegant 100-room Mayfair Manor opened at 237 North Tryon Street, an apartment hotel designed by Louis Asbury Sr. Fifty rooms were for travelers and fifty reserved for permanent residents, including one of the owners who lived on the top floor. Built by Dr. J. P. Matheson and Dr. C. N. Peeler of Charlotte, two of the founders of the Charlotte Eye, Ear, Nose, and Throat Hospital a block away, it was an ambitious but relatively small, privately owned hotel in which every room had a bath, phone, and radio. Very modern! Also, guests received golf privileges at the Myers Park Country Club. Surrounded by small shops and large department stores, the ten-story hotel was built on the site of the Tryon Street Methodist Episcopal Church at the corner of Sixth and North Tryon Streets. The sand-colored brick and cast-stone facade rose to a marble-floored penthouse suite and narrow ornate balcony. In the lobby, walnut woodwork and bronze fixtures surrounded a large open fireplace. In 1929, fifteen hotels served uptown Charlotte. By the 1960s, Mayfair became the James Lee Motor Inn. It was sold again, and a second major renovation created the Dunhill Hotel, reopening in 1988 with sixty rooms. The Dunhill became a Charlotte-Mecklenburg Historic Landmark in 1989, and in 1991 it was listed as one of the National Trust's seventy-five Historic Hotels of America.*

Hotel Alexander, Charlotte, N. C.

S & W CAFETERIA. CHARLOTTE, N. C.   103

Hotel Alexander. *At 513 North McDowell at Ninth Street, this three-story white frame building was advertised on the back of this postcard as "one of the Nation's Finest and most Exclusive and Newest Negro Hotels." Newspapers reported, "Dr. J. Eugene Alexander, a Negro physician, bought the old home [1946] and turned it into a hotel for Negroes. His wife Bobbie ran it." During the years of segregated hotels, this one in the 1940s and 1950s welcomed big bands, entertainers such as Louis "Satchmo" Armstrong, businessmen and other travelers, and it served as a center for the First Ward community. Predating the Alexander were other uptown hotels for blacks in First, Second and Third Wards: Sanders Hotel, Goode Hotel, Little Ponce de Leon, and the Hotel Williams designed by Louis Asbury Sr. The building that Hotel Alexander occupied had been built and dedicated in 1905 as the Florence Crittenton Home. Wealthy New York druggist Charles Crittenton built it as one of sixty such homes he founded as a "Home for Fallen Women" for "shelter and protection to young girls when the first misstep is made." Ironically the dedication ceremony platform itself fell when it became overloaded with local dignitaries. Architects Wheeler, Runge, and Dickie donated plans for the home which had seven pleasant, airy bedrooms, a sewing room, a nursery, and an infirmary. It served through 1946 and moved on January 1, 1947. The building became a hotel in use until legislation desegregated hotels. Firefighters supervised the burning of the structure in 1973.*

S & W Cafeteria. *There is hardly a better remembered institution in Charlotte than the S & W. When teenager Frank Sherrill left his job as an Ivey's department store window trimmer and went to California, he returned with an idea new to the South in the 1920s, but familiar in California—cafeterias. He and Fred Webber began the Southeast's pioneer chain of cafeterias. Charlotte's S & W opened in 1920, then moved next door to this larger cafeteria pictured at 116 West Trade Street. Sherrill envisioned good food and low prices, with the quality and flavor of "an extension of the boarding house." In 1937, their steak and french fries were thirty-five cents. Peach shortcake cost a dime. This S & W was Charlotteans' favorite place to eat for many decades, closing in 1970. In 1932, Architect Martin E. Boyer Jr. drew plans for the remodeled interior (pictured here) with a terrazzo fountain, high ceilings, and balconies in Art Moderne style, designed after Peacock Alley at New York's Waldorf Astoria. Sherrill became a multimillionaire via his many ventures and owned Bald Head Island for more than thirty years. (Courtesy Charlotte Museum of History and Hezekiah Alexander Homesite)*

5—WM. R. BARRINGER HOTEL, CHARLOTTE, N. C.

Barringer Hotel. *In the 1940–50s, visiting celebrities such as Judy Garland, Gloria Swanson, Richard Nixon, and Tyrone Power stayed at the ritzy, 350-room Barringer Hotel. Owners Laurence and Flora Barringer named the hotel for their father, William R. Barringer, adding it to the chain of hotels Laurence owned in the Carolinas and Georgia. The Charlotte News dubbed him a "hotel baron." When it opened in 1940, the original twelve-story hotel at 426 North Tryon Street had 200 rooms in a plan drawn by Dial and Thomas of Columbia and Miami. Room capacity increased by 150 about 1950 with a twelve-story rear addition designed by Leonard Schultze of New York. One hundred percent air conditioned meant it had the newest boon to the South, cool rooms in summer. In the lobby, spread with oriental rugs, twelve bellmen lined up daily for inspection. The hotel's name changed to the Cavalier Inn, which closed in 1975. Subsequently named Hall House, it became a residence for the elderly. This site had earlier held the home and office of Dr. Annie Alexander, the region's first licensed female doctor. She graduated from the Women's Medical College in Philadelphia in 1884.*

6. Where We Worshipped *Churches*

Charlotte, N. C., The Industrial Center of the   New South. Episcopal Church

St. Peter's Episcopal. *This mother church of area Episcopal churches was completed in 1893 at the corner of North Tryon and West Seventh Streets, where the vigorous congregation continues. From 1858 to 1890, the church occupied an earlier structure on the same site. Prior to this, the congregation held services in the town's community church (later the site of First Presbyterian), then built a small brick church in 1846 on West Trade Street, across from the U.S. Mint. The church pictured is made of dark brick and red mortar, with brown stone detail; it is cruciform in shape and provincial English Gothic in style, with large clerestory windows. During the Civil War, members shipped cotton via blockade runners to purchase Bibles and prayer books from England for Confederate soldiers. A Confederate seal can be found in one of the sanctuary windows. St. Peter's Episcopal Church fostered three Charlotte institutions: St. Peter's Hospital, 1876; Thompson Orphanage, 1887; and Good Samaritan Hospital, 1888. The Parish Hall built in 1911–12 housed an active soup kitchen for the homeless for many years.*

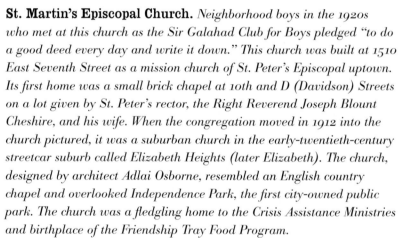

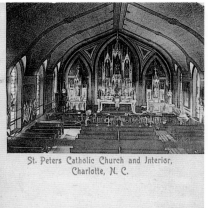

St. Peters Catholic Church and Interior,
Charlotte, N. C.

St. Martin's Episcopal Church. *Neighborhood boys in the 1920s who met at this church as the Sir Galahad Club for Boys pledged "to do a good deed every day and write it down." This church was built at 1510 East Seventh Street as a mission church of St. Peter's Episcopal uptown. Its first home was a small brick chapel at 10th and D (Davidson) Streets on a lot given by St. Peter's rector, the Right Reverend Joseph Blount Cheshire, and his wife. When the congregation moved in 1912 into the church pictured, it was a suburban church in the early-twentieth-century streetcar suburb called Elizabeth Heights (later Elizabeth). The church, designed by architect Adlai Osborne, resembled an English country chapel and overlooked Independence Park, the first city-owned public park. The church was a fledgling home to the Crisis Assistance Ministries and birthplace of the Friendship Tray Food Program.*

St. Peter's Catholic Church. *This St. Peter's Catholic Church built in 1893 replaced an earlier church dedicated in 1852. Visits by Catholic priests to Charlotte Catholics began in 1824, perhaps to provide services for goldminers as well as residents. The handsome Victorian rectory (right of the church) was built in 1897. On the remodeled sanctuary's plaster altar wall, noted artist Ben Long completed in 1989 a large fresco in three parts: "The Agony in the Garden," "Pentecost," and "Resurrection." The church is located at 507 South Tryon Street.*

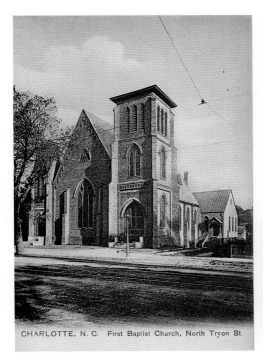

CHARLOTTE, N. C. First Baptist Church, North Tryon St.

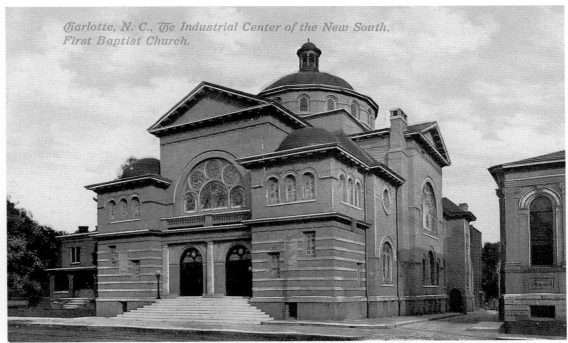

Charlotte, N. C., The Industrial Center of the New South.
First Baptist Church.

First Baptist Church. *Prior to the church pictured, Charlotte Baptists built their first town church in 1833, named Beulah Baptist Church, located on the northwest corner of College and Third Streets. In 1857, a second building was erected on the southeast corner of Brevard and Seventh Streets called the Charlotte Baptist Church of Christ. The third building, Tryon Street Baptist Church (pictured here), was constructed in 1884 at 318 North Tryon Street. Architect A. L. West of Richmond, Virginia, was paid $115 for his design plans and specifications. A steeple was added later. The fourth home of the congregation was completed in 1909 on the same North Tryon Street site. The picture used for this postcard appeared in 1896 publications.*

First Baptist Church. *In the spring of 1906, members of the First Baptist Church agreed that growth demanded a larger church building to replace their current building at 318 North Tryon Street. They chose popular church architect and member James Mackson McMichael, and "the byzantine architectural scheme emphasizing the central dome effect was adopted." Andrew Carnegie had offered $5,000 for the purchase of a pipe organ contingent upon the church's choosing an architectural style compatible with the new Carnegie public library next door on North Tryon Street. It is reported that he was so pleased with the finished church's design that he paid the full bill for the organ. The church was dedicated in 1909. Dr. Luther Little, minister, pioneered his radio ministry broadcasts here beginning in 1921. The building served the First Baptist congregation until 1975, when the building was sold to Mecklenburg County for an arts and performance center. The magnificent stained-glass windows and elegant architectural details have remained intact. Renamed in 1997, it became Spirit Square Center for Arts and Education, and its handsome domed sanctuary was renamed McGlohon Performance Place after nationally known jazz musician-composer Loonis McGlohon of Charlotte. It became a Charlotte-Mecklenburg Historic Landmark in 1976.*

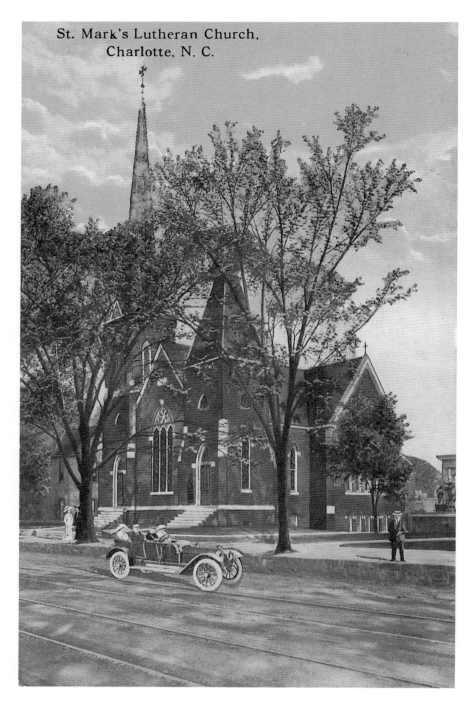

St. Mark's Lutheran Church,
Charlotte, N. C.

St. Mark's Lutheran Church. *The towering steeple on the east side at 414 North Tryon Street was a familiar landmark announcing Charlotte's third Lutheran church building, completed in 1890. Lutherans were early settlers of Mecklenburg's bordering counties, such as Cabarrus, where they operated Mt. Pleasant Collegiate Institute. St. Mark's Lutheran Church was organized at the First Presbyterian Church in 1859. This notable "mother church" of Charlotte Lutheranism (pictured here) remained in use until the congregation moved in 1960 to Queens and Edgehill Roads. The earlier building was sold by the Lutheran Church to the neighboring Barringer Hotel for its expansion.*

Charlotte, N. C. Tryon Street M. E. Church, South.

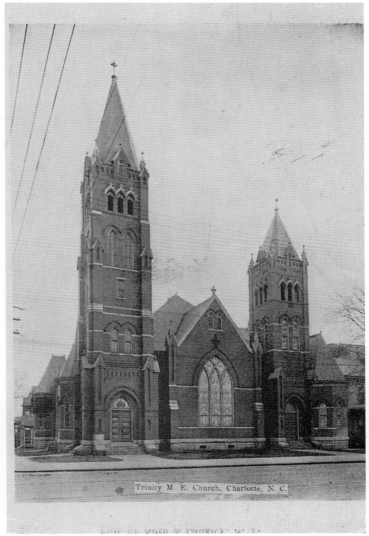

Trinity M. E. Church, Charlotte, N. C.

A Charlotte newspaper reported in 1891 that the Tryon Street Methodist Episcopal Church at 235 North Tryon Street at the corner of West Sixth Street would rebuild on the site and the new facility would have a "main audience room" with "cathedral galleries, arched and pillared," and classrooms. When rebuilt that year, the two-story church looked as it does in this picture, with the striking needle-like steeple visible in many bird's-eye views of North Tryon Street looking toward Fourth Ward. Note the

pastor's residence next door at 233 North Tryon Street, which in 1902 was occupied by the Reverend H. F. Chreitzberg. Earlier buildings for the Tryon Street church had occupied this same corner beginning in 1859. In 1927, this church merged with a daughter congregation, Trinity Methodist Episcopal, which had organized in 1896 at 401 South Tryon Street. Once the two congregations combined, they moved up Tryon Street to become First United Methodist Church.

FIRST METHODIST EPISCOPAL CHURCH, CHARLOTTE, N. C.

First Methodist Episcopal Church. *Two large uptown Methodist churches, one called Trinity, the other named Tryon Street, anchored opposite ends of Tryon Street, but combined in 1927 to build this impressive, modified Gothic church at 501 North Tryon Street. The congregations felt that together they could better accomplish their goals. Architect Edwin Brewster Phillips of Memphis, Tennessee, designed the structure with buttressed towers and an interior sanctuary in the Gothic mode, seating 1,560. The left tower contains a set of twenty Deagan chimes. Indiana limestone faces the entire building. Tobacco tycoon James B. Duke, a Methodist, promised before his death in 1925 to contribute $100,000 to the church, and his daughter Doris fulfilled his verbal pledge in 1934. During the years 1927–39, the church was named First Methodist Episcopal, South. In 1939, it dropped "South" from its name, then became First United Methodist Church in 1968.*

Hawthorne Lane Methodist Church. *Prominent architect Louis Asbury Sr. designed this brick church, which held its first service at 501 Hawthorne Lane at Eighth Street. The congregation had formally organized in 1915, meeting in the Elizabeth College chapel, and was welcomed as a neighborhood church in Elizabeth. Textile mill owner B. D. Heath gave the lot, and J. A. Jones Construction Co. built the church for about $50,000 in 1916. In 1993, the church became a designated Charlotte-Mecklenburg Historic Landmark. It is an intact example of an Akron-plan Gothic Revival church of the early twentieth century. Interior craftsmanship includes a stained-glass window showing a preaching scene with John Wesley, founder of Methodism in England. Department store owner Joseph Benjamin Ivey was a charter member and a longtime Sunday school superintendent. The church later became Hawthorne Lane United Methodist Church.*

East Avenue Tabernacle. *When the East Avenue Associate Reformed Presbyterian Church was built in 1914, it was surrounded by a dense, thriving residential neighborhood. Situated on a point where Trade Street (East Avenue) split, going down one flank of the church and Elizabeth Avenue on the other flank, it was in a prime location at 926 Elizabeth Avenue. The congregation, organized in 1899, moved from a nearby building into this fine brick sanctuary designed by premier church architect J. M. McMichael. It features McMichael's trademarks: a large, circular sanctuary with a dome and balcony, and a neoclassical entrance. In 1917, the congregation still couldn't afford stained-glass windows for the sanctuary, but the Reverend W. W. Orr dug into his pocket for $2,700 for dozens of elegant stained-glass windows of biblical scenes. In 1925, a rear addition was designed by McMichael. The diminishing congregation voted in 1992 to sell the building. Later, they joined Craig Avenue A.R.P. Church. Philanthropist Bruce Parker's 1997 purchase and renovation of the East Avenue Tabernacle created the Great Aunt Stella Center which opened in 1998, housing a charter school, community service groups, the Parker Foundation, and a wide range of performances. The renamed building is a memorial to the remarkable charitable spirit of Stella V. Sparrow, the great-aunt of Parker.*

First Presbyterian Church. *When workmen in 1883–84 nimbly built this replacement steeple on the town ridgeline at 200 West Trade Street, they claimed that from its 182½-foot height on clear days, they could see the Blue Ridge Mountains and Virginia's Peaks of Otter. To build it, men pulled the old steeple down, heaving on a long rope stretched from the steeple across West Trade Street. This site first housed a town church dedicated in 1823 to serve all denominations. The town cemetery, used from the 1770s and later called Settlers' Cemetery, was also on the site. The town church became First Presbyterian in 1835. Plans were made in 1851 to build a larger church, which was completed in 1857. Early building costs were met by selling deeds for pews. In 1871, General Rufus Barringer bought pew 33 for $25. Until the practice ceased, pews often remained in families or were resold to newcomers. Pews with brass nameplates are those of Governor Zeb Vance, Mrs. Stonewall Jackson, Confederate general D. H. Hill, John Irwin, Harriet Vance, and the Reverend Walter M. Moore. The steeple of that 1857 structure had a silver trumpet mounted on top (called Gabriel's Trumpet), placed there by a daring young deacon, Patrick J. Lowrie. The Reverend Robert Hall Morrison, Mrs. Stonewall Jackson's father, was the first called minister in 1827. The postcard view shows what remains of the 1857 building: entrance facade, narthex, and foundation of the bell tower. In 1895, a new sanctuary was built. The church still stands in a parklike setting in uptown Charlotte. It was placed on the National Register of Historic Places in 1982.*

CHARLOTTE, N. C.   First Presbyterian Church   5084

Charlotte, N. C.,
View of Second Presbyterian Church.

Second Presbyterian Church. *As Charlotte grew in the 1870s, Presbyterian newcomers found that the pews at the only town church of that denomination were already owned, inherited, and occupied by its members, as was the custom. Consequently, the crowded congregation of First Presbyterian organized a second church in 1873. They met in the county courthouse until they could afford to build. By 1875, a church was completed, but it became too small less than two decades later. They decided to build again. Finally, in September 1892, when this new building at 214 North Tryon Street was finished and ready to be occupied, the 600 members celebrated. The 64' × 80' red-carpeted sanctuary had seats for 800 with use of adjoining Sunday school rooms, a raised choir loft, a large pipe organ behind the pulpit, and a handsome stamped-steel design on the vaulted ceiling. One hundred and twenty gas jets lit the chandeliers. Bricks in the rounded corners of the church tower were laid by J. A. Jones, a young mason from Anson County who went on to build one of the world's largest construction companies. In 1947, the seventy-four-year-old congregation united with Westminster Church to form Covenant Presbyterian Church. It was built in Dilworth at 1000 East Morehead Street.*

First Baptist Church, Lumberton, N. C.

Because so few postcards exist of early-twentieth-century African American churches or buildings, this postcard depicting a Lumberton, North Carolina, church is notable and included here because it closely resembles Charlotte's important Little Rock A.M.E. Zion Church, completed in June 1911. The First Baptist Church in Lumberton (pictured) opened in 1910. Both are still standing in their original locations in different parts of the state. The Charlotte church began in the early 1870s when freed slaves first had the opportunity to form their own churches and hear their own preachers. Black members raised the entire $20,000 for the brick Charlotte church. J. M. McMichael, the leading architect of affluent white churches in the region, designed it. The building, located at 403 North Myers Street, reopened in March 1986 as the Afro-American Cultural Center. It became a Charlotte-Mecklenburg Historic Landmark in 1982. (Courtesy Sarah Manning Pope Collection).

7. Doing Business *Commercial, Industry, Textiles*

Manufacturers Club and Observer Building, Charlotte, N. C.

Southern Manufacturers' Club and Charlotte Daily Observer. *This was one of Charlotte's most historic buildings, the city's last identifiable link with the Civil War and Reconstruction, altered significantly, then razed in 1973. The three-story Charlotte Branch of the Bank of North Carolina at 122 South Tryon Street was built before 1860 and was used for one of the last cabinet meetings of the Confederacy in April 1865. Subsequently the bank failed following the financial panic of 1873, and the building was home to the Charlotte Daily Observer from 1893 to 1916. The Chronicle was the Observer's afternoon publication. In this "Observer building," the group organized by New South activist D. A. Tompkins founded the influential Southern Manufacturers' Club in 1894. Tompkins's partner was Joseph P. Caldwell, the Observer editor who became one of North Carolina's greatest newspaper editors. With an invited membership of 100 in 1902, the Club operated at this site in twenty-two rooms before constructing an imposing new club in 1910 at 300 West Trade Street. The fourth story was added after 1899. On the roof gleams Charlotte's first lighted sign.*

What an outcry when the Realty/
Independence Building went up in 1908–9,
and again in 1981 when it came down in
seven seconds. This first steel-frame skyscraper in the Carolinas, at 102 West Trade
Street, replaced a favorite drugstore housed
in a landmark frame house (Osborne's
Corner). The 1981 implosion created space
for modern high-rise offices. At the beginning of the twentieth century, skyscraper
was a popular term for a building more
than ten stories high. Once this building
opened, Charlotte was quite proud of the
twelve-story symbol of the city's New South
progress. Designed in Sullivanesque style
by Frank Milburn of Washington, D.C., and
contracted by J. A. Jones Construction Co.,
it housed a street-level bank and drugstore,
and upstairs offices of lawyers, dentists, insurance companies, architects, and numerous doctors, including as a first tenant the
founder of the Nalle Clinic. The Carolinas'
first radio station, WBT, was licensed to
operate on 100 watts and opened studios
here in 1922. The structure was renamed
the Independence Building when the Independence Trust Co. opened a bank on its
first two floors. The bank failed during the
Great Depression, but the name stuck. In
1928, New York architect W. L. Stoddart
designed two additional floors and the
building lost its elegant, original cornice.
When the building opened, a reporter wrote,
"The views from the higher floors are fine.
The people there are on even terms with
the city dragon" (the stylized weathervane
atop the nearby City Hall).

CHARLOTTE'S HEAD SPECIALTY SHOP

Hancock and Wishart Barber Shop. *During the Realty Building's early years, this barber shop on the seventh floor advertised with postcards (postmark 1912), proud to be "Charlotte's Head Specialty Shop."*

A later shop called Hancock's was in the basement and offered modern methods and equipment, hot and cold shower baths, manicures, and a hair-dressing parlor.

The Mercantile Heart of Charlotte

(Ivey's, S. H. Kress & Co., and Yorke Bros. & Rogers). Founded in 1900, Ivey's grew steadily at a series of uptown locations. The first store (not pictured) was in the second block of North Tryon Street, near Sixth Street. Founder J. B. Ivey opened his second store (pictured here) in the first block of West Trade Street, next to S. H. Kress & Co. He recruited his neighboring business owner, David Ovens, as his general manager.

Employees of the J. B. Ivey Co. on a trolley ride.

Mr. Ivey scheduled annual outings for employees, sometimes to Cleveland County where he had grown up and earned his first mercantile experience in a cotton mill store. The trolley's banner advertised: "It Will Pay to Trade at Ivey's Tomorrow."

VIEW ON NORTH TRYON STREET, CHARLOTTE, N. C.

View on North Tryon Street, Charlotte.
The third Ivey's store was located just north of the Independence Building. It was here that Frank Sherrill and Fred Webber, who later cofounded S & W Cafeterias, managed the lunch counter.

J. B. IVEY & COMPANY DEPARTMENT STORE, CHARLOTTE, N. C.   B-801

J. B. Ivey & Co. Department Store. *In 1923–24, the J. B. Ivey Co. built at 127 North Tryon Street one of the Southeast's most elegant department stores designed by Charlotte architect W. H. Peeps. Ivey was a Methodist minister's son who pulled dark shades to cover his store windows on Sundays. The building was later expanded to the rear. This store closed in 1990, then reopened with sixty-two residential condominiums in 1995.*

Old Osborne Corner. *In late-nineteenth-century Charlotte, folks called this white-frame, gabled residence on the northwest corner of Trade and Tryon Streets "the Old Osborne Corner," after the family of lawyer, editor, and former Mint assayer James W. Osborne. Built in the 1800s for John Irwin, it straddles the earlier era when there were more homes than shops in the uptown blocks. By 1900, this corner had become a busy but rustic mercantile center. The anchoring corner house held a tailor's shop and office upstairs and was remodeled at street level for the Woodall and Sheppard Drugstore, which also, as the sign announces, sold paints and glass. Customers entered from West Trade Street to quench their thirst at the "magnificent fountain of fluted Mexican onyx, mahogany, stained glass scenic panels, and a row of electric rosettes." The fountain and its broad mirror were designed by Becker-Iceless Soda Fountains of Cleveland, Ohio. Shops left and right of the drugstore sold dry goods, clothes, furniture, pianos, millinery, fruit, jewelry, and plumbing fixtures. Another drugstore was virtually next door (right), and still others (not shown) sat on opposite corners. The Independence Building followed by the Independence Center and the Marriott City Center replaced what is pictured.*

379. Old Osborne Corner, now occupied by Sky Scrapers.   Published by C. H. Robinson & Co.

Charlotte, N. C.—East Trade Street
STONE & BARRINGER CO.

MILL NEWS PRINT, CHARLOTTE

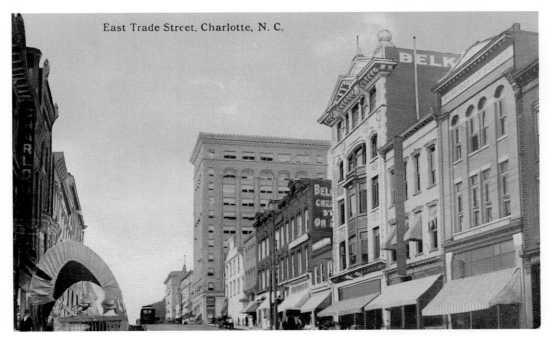

East Trade Street, Charlotte, N. C.

East Trade Street, Charlotte. *Young William Henry Belk worked twelve years in his hometown of Monroe, until he earned $750 to start his own business. He and his brother opened a department store on East Trade Street in Charlotte in 1895. Belk rented successive storefronts until, in 1909–10, he built a handsome five-story store at 115 East Trade Street. It was designed by Wheeler and Stern, an architectural firm with offices in New York and Charlotte. A newspaper reported that the facade was of French Renaissance style. The store contained 47,000 feet of floor space. Charlotteans recall that farmers brought mountain apples to sell from their wagons (left) along Trade Street. The store was much enlarged in 1927, and by the 1940s Belk's became an extensive southern chain of more than 200 stores. The Charlotte store absorbed rival Efird's and expanded to Fifth Street. The Protestants had cornered the department store market. The Belks were Presbyterians, the Iveys Methodists, and the Efirds Baptists. Belk vacated uptown in 1988, the building was demolished in 1989, and the three connected buildings were replaced by NationsBank Corporate Center (now Bank of America), Founders Hall, and the North Carolina Blumenthal Center for the Arts.*

EFIRD'S DEPARTMENT STORE. CHARLOTTE. N. C.   104

Efird's Department Store. *Remembered by thousands of Charlotte residents for its escalator, the first moving stairs in the region, folks also came from far-flung farms and mill villages to uptown Charlotte where Efird's, Belk's, and Ivey's formed a star trio for shopping. Opened in September 1924 at 127 North Tryon Street at a cost of $700,000, the elegant neoclassical Efird's building was designed by architect Louis Asbury Sr., an MIT graduate who was Charlotte's first major native architect. An earlier store had until 1907 been known as the Bee Hive and as Charlotte Mercantile Co., owned and run by members of the local Efird family who hailed from Anson County. In 1909, Efird's had a huge sale in ladies clothing, straw hats, Octagon Soap, Gail & Ax Snuff, colorful parasols, lace curtains, and Marseilles bedspreads. In 1913, they had branch stores in Concord, Gastonia, and Winston-Salem. In the 1950s, the fifty-eight-store Efird's chain was bought by Belk.*

Jordan's Drugstore. *In this excellent 1908 view of Jordan's Drugstore on the northwest corner of the Square, note the tall, ornate soda fountain along the rear wall. Popular Jordan's also sold candies, cigars, card cases, and collar and cuff boxes, and traded in politics as well. Their ad promised "no short weights" of prescription amounts. Owner Robert Henry Jordan sent medicine free of charge to those in need. The handsome masonry building Jordan's occupied during the years 1884–1918 was actually a residence-store combination known as Springs' Corner. It was owned by John Springs III of Fort Mill, who used the upstairs as a residence when in Charlotte. Brevard Davidson and Davidson College subsequently owned the corner, which retained a drugstore later called Liggett's in a new building until Bank of America (formerly NationsBank) Corporate Center and Founders Hall occupied the site in the 1990s.*

Bowen's. *When John Bowen opened his drugstore in 1911 at 1 South Tryon Street, he enjoyed a prime location on the southeast corner of the Square. Patrons could order ice cream sodas, lemonade, or sarsparilla from the soda fountain counter (right), with its big mirror and lights above the large cash register. Each table had pull-out seats for customers. After their thirst was satisfied, customers might buy toiletries or medicine from the long wall of display shelves (left and rear right). Note the patterned decorative ceiling of pressed tin, the handsome marble counter, and the bordered tile floor. John Bowen ran the store with N. J. Bowen as bookkeeper. By 1913–14, John Bowen had a second drugstore at 9 North Graham Street. Prior to Bowen's proprietorship, previous drugstores on the 1 South Tryon site were Atkinson's (1908) and Hamilton-Martin Drug (1909). The space later became Bank of America Plaza.*

BROCKMANN'S, CHARLOTTE, N. C. "A BOOK STORE OF RARE EXCELLENCE."

Charlotte, N.C.
The Industrial
Centre of the
New South.

Stone & Barringer Co.
Booksellers, Stationers,
Office Outfitters.

Brockmann's Book Store. *When the Academy of Music building burned on December 17, 1922, fire also destroyed the three-story Brockmann's Book Store building next door at 210 South Tryon Street. Brockmann-Legerton Co., Inc., was a vital uptown institution begun in 1916, becoming Brockmann and Co. in 1917. Charles Brockmann joined the company in 1917 when his brother began World War I military service. After the 1922 fire, John R. Scott, the building's owner, rebuilt immediately on the same site and Brockmann's occupied the street-level space of the new four-story building designed by C. C. Hook. The shop sold books, stationery, toys and novelties, magazines, office supplies, and services such as framing and engraving, and it offered a circulating library. Brockmann's continued until 1927. Charles Brockmann was subsequently with the Community Book Shop at 6 West Fifth Street, was assistant director of the Charlotte Public Library, and coauthored* Hornets' Nest: The Story of Charlotte and Mecklenburg County *(1961) with Legette Blythe.*

Stone and Barringer. *This may look like a modest bookstore, but its civic role was vital to the town. Prior to 1901, the Charlotte Literary and Library Association, which became the public library, was located in an upstairs room of the four-story Stone and Barringer bookstore at 22 South Tryon Street. In 1891, a subscription library with a librarian had been incorporated. In 1902, the YWCA was formally organized here. Charles S. Stone, bookstore president and treasurer, ran the business from about 1899 to 1919, selling books, stationery, and art supplies. The bookstore also served as publisher of books by poet and journalist John Charles McNeill, among other Charlotte writers.*

American Trust Building,
Charlotte, N. C.

A3069

American Trust Co. *Organizers had high ambitions when they started the Southern States Trust in 1901, soon changing its name to American Trust Co. The bank would grow regionally and later become Bank of America. The building at 206 South Tryon Street was designed by Hoggson Bros. of New York, which specialized in bank design. Bank offices and operations on the first two floors included a committee room "for the use of ladies who are customers of the bank and their friends who may wish to have meetings up town." The room had desks, stationery, and access to a stenographer who could be summoned as needed.*

The main banking room was 50' × 60' with a 29-foot ceiling, mahogany furniture, marble mosaic floors, and counters and screens of mahogany and bronze. The site was the former YMCA building, and some portions of that building were incorporated into this "American Building" which opened in 1909 with an American flag flying above the granite-based terra cotta facade. At its fiftieth anniversary in 1951, the bank called itself "The Country Bank That Went to Town."

COMMERCIAL NATIONAL BANK BUILDING, CHARLOTTE, N. C.

COMMERCIAL NATIONAL BANK DRIVE-IN BRANCH, 135 WEST MOREHEAD STREET, CHARLOTTE, N. C.

Commercial National Bank. *Twelve stories of marble and terra cotta, brick and steel, this bank building had room for 170 offices at 200 South Tryon Street. When it was completed in 1913 and nicknamed the city's "second skyscraper," this substantial building cost about $285,000 and was a symbol of financial stability. The contractor was Whitney-Steen Co. When many banks failed to reopen in 1933 after the depression-era Bank Holiday, Commercial National held strong. Chartered in 1874, it merged with American Trust in 1957 and in 1960 became North Carolina National Bank (later Bank of America). Commercial National was the first in the state to open a drive-in branch (1948).*

Charlotte, N. C.—South Tryon Street.

Piedmont Building (first building on left). *Built in 1898, this imposing office building at 220 South Tryon Street housed the offices of the 4C's Company (Charlotte Consolidated Construction Company, which built Dilworth, the streetcar line, and other important turn-of-the-twentieth-century projects). Offices in the building housed lawyers, the Law Library, insurance agents, and real estate salesmen, as well as meeting rooms of the Masons prior to the building of the Masonic Temple. The modern Charlotte Chamber of Commerce was organized in the Piedmont Building in 1905 as the Greater Charlotte Club. The Piedmont was considered Charlotte's original skyscraper, soon to be surpassed by the much taller Independence Building in 1908. Designed by architect Frank Milburn and advertised prior to 1900 as the "finest commercial building in N.C.," it was razed in 1956.*

Professional Bldg., N. Tryon and 7th St., Charlotte, N. C.—37

Professional Building. *In the 1920s, when medical offices clustered uptown around several Charlotte hospitals, a group of prominent physicians and dentists formed a cooperative plan for a large Professional Building. This was built in 1923 for $300,000 by the J. A. Jones Construction Co. at 403 North Tryon Street at the corner of West Seventh and North Tryon Streets. Architect Louis Asbury Sr. designed the eight-story building which had street-level stores for medical/surgical supplies, a basement barber shop and restaurant, and, on the upper floors, suites for physicians, dentists, surgeons, and others. Several blocks away were both St. Peter's Hospital and the private Charlotte Sanatorium. The handsome exterior was of pale yellow brick with granite base and limestone trim. When physicians and hospitals gradually moved to the outskirts, the building was converted for business. Even in 1989, before the building was demolished in 1995, the original Otis elevators from 1923 were still in use, hand-operated by a genial gentleman who greeted and took riders to their floors. The building occupied one corner of the site which subsequently became TransAmerica Square (1997).*

The C. W. Johnston Bldg., Charlotte, N. C.—38

Johnston Building. *This elegant office building that cotton built in 1924 is a monument to industrialist Charles Worth Johnston and prosperity from his controlling interest in Highland Park Manufacturing Co. and the Johnston Mill in North Charlotte and the Anchor Mills in Huntersville. Designed by New York architect W. L. Stoddart, the fifteen-story building's front face is of limestone with handsome entry and marble lobby details. The building at 212 South Tryon Street advertised the textile success of the New South. The owners and the architect were also proud of the building's "four elevators, with a guaranteed speed of 600 feet per minute." Former governor Cameron Morrison had his law office on the eleventh floor, and the fledgling Duke Endowment occupied fourth-floor offices. New owners made extensive renovations in the early 1980s. In 1992, it became a Charlotte-Mecklenburg Historic Landmark.*

C-30:—THE WILDER BUILDING, CHARLOTTE, N. C.

27848

Wilder Building. *The ten-story Wilder Building of brick and terra cotta tile at 237 South Tryon Street was erected in 1925–26 and designed by architect W. G. Rogers. Sarah D. Worsham Wilder lived in the tenth-story penthouse. She had insisted on this before agreeing to permit construction on the tract where she and her late husband, Dr. Hillory M. Wilder, had lived. Dr. Wilder, a noted surgeon, was county physician for twenty years and later city physician, spending fifty years in the practice of medicine and surgery in the era before specialization. Educated at New York University and at postgraduate clinics in Guy's Hospital in London, he had also served as physician for a time on a British Merchant Marine transatlantic steamer, was a Charlotte alderman, and was instrumental in founding and planning surgical areas of Charlotte's Mercy Hospital. His daughter's will directed 70 percent of the proceeds go to a Charlotte hospital or medical scholarships. Until the building was razed in 1983, it held offices. One notable early tenant was WBT radio. Later, WBTV made a pioneering live TV broadcast from the rooftop.*

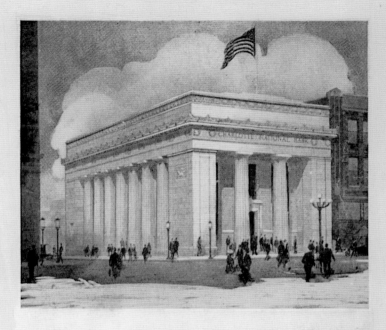

Facts Concerning the New Building of the

CHARLOTTE NATIONAL BANK

The Greek Doric columns which surround the bank weigh 26 tons each and are the largest columns of any bank in the Virginias or Carolinas.

Upon the frieze of the bank there are replicas of famous coins.

The height of the ceiling from floor to dome is 42 feet.

The interior is finished in tavernelle claire marble and Caen stone with a Tennessee marble floor.

The vault has a circular steel door 82 inches in diameter, the steel work of the vault weighing 95,000 pounds, the door alone weighing 33,000 pounds.

One of the features of the new building is an attractive Ladies' Room with complete appointments.

Charlotte National Bank. *New York architect Alfred Charles Bossom, a native of England, said at the bank's opening in 1919 that this building was one of the most satisfactory results in his 26 years as an architect. Builder C. T. Wills, Inc., of New York had to get permission from the war industries board since the building was begun during World War I when materials and labor were scarce. It cost $150,000. Stonework was overseen by John J. Morton, one of the best stone contractors in the South. The pristine classical-design building with marble Doric columns presided like a Greek temple on the northwest corner of South Tryon and West Fourth Streets. Replicas of famous coins ornamented the frieze, and lion-head spouts and stylized flowers embellished the entablature. After designing many southeastern banks while residing in the United States (1903–26), the architect returned to England, became a member of Parliament, and received the title Lord Bossom of Maidstone. In 1939, Charlotte National Bank merged with Wachovia Bank and Trust and used this building until 1958. The property was purchased, then used by First Citizens Bank and Trust beginning in 1960, until the site was cleared for First Citizen's new $50 million bank building and office tower. Key ornamental elements, including some columns pictured, were relocated for adaptive restoration in 1985 at 428 East Fourth Street for the Charlotte National Building.*

C-4:—FIRST NATIONAL BANK BLDG., CHARLOTTE, N. C.

25573

First National Bank. *This handsome 1927 "skyscraper" at 112 South Tryon Street was the tallest building in the Carolinas until the erection of the Reynolds Building in Winston-Salem. Customers could bank at First National on street level or whiz on the Federal Reserve express to the top-floor offices of the Federal Reserve Bank of Richmond. Designed by Lockwood-Greene Co. and Louis Asbury Sr., the twenty-story tower boasts exuberant details: a huge sandstone entry arch hand-carved in place by Italian artisans depicting ornate animals and symbols; gleaming brass chandeliers and elevator doors; and two great cast-iron entry doors whose twenty-four panels represent ancient mythological figures. Although the bank did not survive the Great Depression, the building became successively the Liberty Life, the Baugh, and the Bank of North Carolina building with a false facade erected in 1964. An ambitious $11 million renovation by SYNCO Inc. was completed in 1982, which restored the original entrance and fixtures and replaced major systems. The architectural firm of A. G. Odell was employed and the building was renamed One Tryon Center.*

THIS HOUSE IS BUILT OF COAL

F. & R. COAL & OIL CO. ⌐ 600 S. Cedar St. ⌐ CHARLOTTE, N. C. ⌐ Phone 3-6177

This House Is Built of Coal. *For many years, homeowners heated their houses with coal-burning furnaces and fireplace grates or cooked over coal-fed stoves. To advertise their business, owners of the F & R Coal and Oil Co. in the 600 block of South Cedar Street published this confident postcard message: "We believe in our coal enough to build an office out of it." The eye-catching tile-roofed, coal-walled office was the headquarters for a fleet of red delivery trucks, two of which are pictured on the card. The company, founded in the 1920s, expressed similar confidence in their other products for sale, including "our gasoline, motor and fuel oil, greases, solvent, and kerosene."*

Charlotte, North Carolina.
The Industrial Centre of the New South:
Lawyers Building, Designed and Built by
Hunter and Vaughn, Architects,
Charlotte, N. C.

Lawyers Building. *This prominent third Lawyers Building in uptown Charlotte was conveniently located at 307 South Tryon Street, next to the fourth Courthouse (left behind small trees). In use by 1908, it was designed and built by contractors R. N. Hunter and Luther Vaughan, and housed on the third floor the law library of the Law Library Association of Charlotte. The nucleus of this library had begun prior to this building with lawyers George E. Wilson and Heriot Clarkson, who had lawbooks of older lawyers assessed and gave the lawyers stock in exchange. Each lawyer member owned one share of stock, par value $200. Charlotte's first Lawyers Building, believed to have been built in the 1880s, was at the corner of North Church and West Fifth Streets, behind that era's courthouse which faced West Trade Street. Its second location for about ten years was in the Piedmont Fire Insurance Building. A fourth Law Building sat at 730 East Trade Street from 1928 until 1993, designed by Louis Asbury Sr.*

Coca-Cola Bottling Plant. *This bottling plant at 1401 West Morehead Street with brick and art deco detailed corners featuring molded Coca-Cola bottles was designed by M. R. Marsh and completed in 1930. The site had been the old Wadsworth farm. This headquarters view shows a fleet of trucks ready to deliver green-glass bottles of Cokes, one of the South's most popular products. Interior air vents defrosted the large picture windows so passersby could always see the mechanized bottling process inside. Windowsills were sloped so bottles would slide off if employees tried to set them in the window between sips. Regional headquarters for Coca-Cola remained here until 1974. The building was later remodeled for offices and is on the National Register of Historic Places. In 1988, it became a Charlotte-Mecklenburg Historic Landmark.*

Charlotte Pipe and Foundry. *Charlotte Pipe and Foundry, begun by Willis Frank Dowd, made cast-iron soil pipe and fittings in Dilworth for Eastern Seaboard markets beginning in 1901. The foundry relocated to this 56-acre site on Dowd Road and Clarkson Street in 1907, following a major fire. In 1967, the company began manufacturing plastic drain pipe and fittings in a Union County plant. More than 1,000 people were employed by the company in four different plants in the 1990s.*

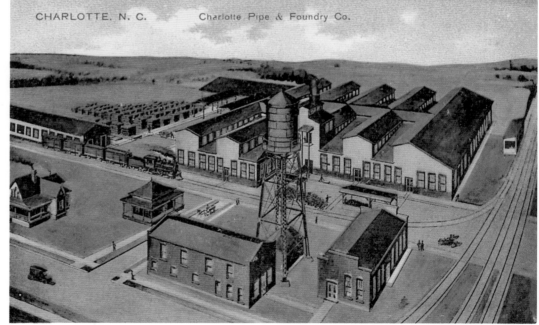

Interstate Granite Corp. *This double-view postcard features the date July 5, 1932, and the company advertisement for "Winnsboro Blue Granite." The upper view shows the building located at the corner of Norris and Hutchison Avenues. Prior to 1931, the business was at 607 West Seventh Street. In the lower view, the company officers stand with their employees. For about forty years, Interstate Granite manufactured for wholesale its standard monumental granite, both finished and semifinished.*

INTERSTATE MILLING CO., THE HOME OF ELIZABETH BEST PATENT FLOUR, CHARLOTTE, N. C.

Interstate Milling. *The large, highly visible Interstate Milling Co. at 620 West Tenth Street in Fourth Ward was its own best billboard, touting popular brands of "high grade flour, meal, and feeds." Incorporated in 1915, the company took advantage of Charlotte rail lines central to thousands of farms and grocery markets. A group of prominent stockholders backed cofounders Charles P. Moody, a wholesale grocer, and George W. Graham Jr. to mill flour for sale to bakeries, groceries, and feed-consuming farms. In 1964, a new elevator and grain facility could transfer 320,000 pounds of grain hourly for rail shipping. The mill with towering grain elevators is clearly visible from Brookshire Freeway. ADM Milling Co. purchased it from J. J. Vanier of Kansas in 1970 and continues operations. (Courtesy Lake County Museum Illinois, Curt Teich Postcard Archives)*

KING COTTON.
An illustration from "Lyrics from Cotton Land", by John Charles McNeil.
Published and Copyrighted by Stone Publishing Co., Charlotte, N. C.

1816 Cotton Field with Pickers near Charlotte, N. C.   W. T. Rowland, Publisher.

Raw cotton flowed into Charlotte by wagon, truck, and rail and left as yarn, gingham, and sheeting, or as bales of compressed cotton. Charlotte was one of the most productive mill towns in the South. Spring and summer rainfall and a dry autumn (cotton-picking time) created an ideal climate for raising cotton.

The region was primarily rural in the first half of the twentieth century when cotton pickers, cotton fields, cotton-laden farm wagons, and bales of ginned cotton awaiting shipment at train platforms were a familiar sight. The postcard "Trucking Cotton on the Old City Platform" is from a photograph dated 1896.

Mecklenburg County Roads near
Charlotte, N. C.

A3063

Mecklenburg County Roads near
Charlotte, N. C.

E 9300 - TRUCKING COTTON ON THE OLD CITY PLATFORM, CHARLOTTE, N.C. THE INDUSTRIAL CENTRE OF THE NEW SOUTH

No. 32335   J. B. Ivey & Co., Publishers   (Germany)

Ye Olden Time Cotton Press, near Charlotte, N. C.

Cotton Industries of Charlotte, N. C.

Cotton Industries of Charlotte. *The Mecklenburg Cotton Mill (top left) opened in November 1904 at 3401 North Davidson Street. Mercury Mills purchased it in 1925 and operated it until 1929. After World War II, the Johnston family purchased the mill. It became a Charlotte-Mecklenburg Landmark in 1987.*

The Highland Park Cotton Mill #1 (top right) opened in 1892 at North Brevard and Sixteenth Streets. It contained 465 looms and produced gingham. W. E. Holt was president and C. W. Johnston was secretary and treasurer.

Two of Charlotte's Twenty Cotton Mills. *The Highland Park Mill #3 (top) opened in 1904. Located at 2901 North Davidson Street, it was Charlotte's most imposing mill with 20,000 spindles, 500 looms, and 800 employees. The spinning and weaving of cotton fiber produced gingham cloth. The plant was designed and constructed by Stuart W. Cramer. To provide recreation for millworkers, the mill owners built Electric Park nearby which included a pond and community center. The mill was designated a Charlotte-Mecklenburg Historic Landmark in 1987.*

Louise Cotton Mill (bottom) opened in 1897 on Hawthorne Lane at the Seaboard Airline Railroad. The mill was named for Louise Chadwick, wife of the company president, H. S. Chadwick. The structure was 90 feet wide and 360 feet long. A major addition was added in 1900.

Highland Park Mill #3 and the Mecklenburg Mill were just two of four large mills clustered on the rail line in North Charlotte. These mills and the close, surrounding mill villages with their shops for millworkers became known on postcards as "The Industrial Centre of the New South."

Model Mill Settlement, Chadwick Mills,
Charlotte, N. C.

Model Mill Settlement, Chadwick Mills. *The Chadwick Mill (1901) was named for H. S. Chadwick. The mill (12,000 spindles, 300 looms) produced yarn and sheeting and was regarded as one of the finest facilities of its kind in the South, with its neat mill houses and landscaping even along the rail line. Mill owners often competed in providing amenities and attracting visitors to their villages. The mill was located by the Seaboard Airline Railroad west of Biddleville.*

Model Mill Settlement, Hoskins, Charlotte, N. C.

Southern Cotton Oil Gin, Pineville, N. C.

Model Mill Settlement, Hoskins. *This mill, which began production in 1904, was located at 201 South Hoskins Road. It was a sister mill of the nearby Chadwick Mill and was owned by the same firm. Residents of the mill houses had room out back for vegetable gardens. The mill was later converted into housing. Hoskins Mill is on the National Register of Historic Places. It became a Charlotte-Mecklenburg Historic Landmark in 1988.*

Southern Cotton Oil Gin. *The life of Charlotte and surrounding towns like Pineville depended on locally grown cotton which farmers brought loose in farm wagons for ginning. Note the finished cotton bale at center ramp. Here seeds were separated from cotton fibers. The seeds were either crushed into cottonseed oil or sent by rail and sold to make lard, soap, candles, and table oil; to pack sardines; or to use as lubricant or illumination in mines. In 1860, cottonseeds were garbage. By 1890, the seeds were highly profitable, thanks to the Southern Cotton Oil Co. and engineer D. A. Tompkins, who had by 1910 helped build 250 cotton oil mills.*

In 1889, the first seasonal bale of cotton to arrive at the Charlotte market was from Pineville, which sent up a hot air balloon in celebration. That bale weighing 460 pounds was bought by cotton broker John VanLandingham for 11¾ cents a pound. J. R. Stroup owned this operation beside the Pineville railroad line in 1914. At one time there were three Pineville gins. The Charlotte News in 1904 called Pineville "the best cotton market" with "a macadamized road and new high bridges . . . greatly facilitating the farmers in hauling their cotton to our town."

TRANQUIL PARK SANITARIUM, CHARLOTTE, N. C.

Tranquil Park Sanitarium. *A brochure advertised a quiet place for healing the mind and body on Selwyn Avenue, "three miles from the City of Charlotte, N.C. on an Asphalt Boulevard passing through Beautiful Myers Park." From about 1916 until 1922, treatments of rest, recreation, and hydrotherapy were offered for noncontagious diseases: "Nervous Affections, Neurasthenia, Exhaustion Psychoses, Simple States of Depression due to business or other stress, and all forms of Chronic Invalidism." Dr. John Q. Myers was the managing director. The site of the former sanitarium is 2800 Selwyn Avenue at Tranquil Avenue. The facility designed by architect Oliver Duke Wheeler was replaced by apartments called Myers Park Manor.*

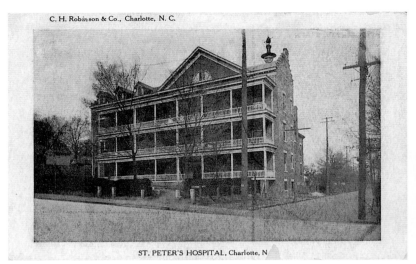

C. H. Robinson & Co., Charlotte, N. C.

ST. PETER'S HOSPITAL, Charlotte, N

Charlotte, N. C.   The Industrial Center of the New South
The Presbyterian Hospital Building

St. Peter's Hospital. *Charlotte's first civilian hospital, known for a time as "St. Peter's Home and Hospital" and "A Hospital with a Soul," existed thirty-one years at various locations before the one pictured on this postcard was built in 1907. It was a twenty-room addition erected in front of an 1898 building. The three-and-a-half-story hospital at 225 North Poplar Street contained a nurses' home, dining room, children's and infants' wards, charity and private rooms on the second floor, and operating and X-ray rooms on the third floor. Episcopal women's wide-ranging efforts had organized the St. Peter's Church Aid Society in 1875. Their first hospital opened two years later in two rented rooms in a house on East Seventh Street. At first, patients to be treated at a hospital had to be almost kidnapped against their or their family's will. Surgery had customarily been performed at patients' homes. In 1940, St. Peter's closed and its patients were transferred to the new Memorial Hospital (now expanded as Carolinas Medical Center). Its porches removed, St. Peter's became the Kenmore Hotel, later renovated for residential condominiums. The exterior was designated a Charlotte-Mecklenburg Historic Landmark in 1978.*

Presbyterian Hospital. *In early 1903, ten physicians headed by J. P. Munroe purchased an existing facility named Charlotte Private Hospital which was established in 1897 as the Medical and Surgical Institute. They placed it under the auspices of white Presbyterian churches and renamed it Presbyterian Hospital. In the early hospital, space was tight, so patients were moved in 1903 to the three-story former Arlington Hotel (known earlier as the Hotel Mecklenburg), 309 West Trade Street (pictured here), on the southeast corner of Mint Street. At this time, Presbyterian was the teaching hospital for the North Carolina Medical College, two blocks away. Medical students could find respite downstairs in the street-level Last Chance Saloon, one of thirteen uptown bars. A memorable physician, Dr. James B. Alexander, managed Presbyterian from 1905 to 1923. It was during his administration the hospital moved to 200 Hawthorne Lane.*

PRESBYTERIAN HOSPITAL, CHARLOTTE, N. C.

Presbyterian Hospital. *In February 1918, Presbyterian Hospital, which had tended patients uptown since 1903, moved to the buildings and twelve acres which had been Elizabeth College at the far end of Elizabeth Avenue at Hawthorne Lane. Presbyterian opened at this site just in time to tend the sick during the Spanish influenza epidemic that crippled the city. In 1940, a large addition was constructed in front of the building pictured. Subsequent additions gradually surrounded it and in 1980 replaced the old building. A carved angel, which is a relic of this original building's facade, has been relocated and inset in a wall of the hospital's interior garden.*

PRESBYTERIAN HOSPITAL, CHARLOTTE, N. C.

Presbyterian Hospital. *To expand at the Hawthorne Lane site, hospital officials and trustees received a $150,000 grant from Duke Endowment to be matched by $300,000 of private funds. In 1940, this new Presbyterian Hospital opened, a state-of-the-art private fireproof hospital, built and furnished for $560,000 to serve the community. The facility relieved the old quarters, the somber Elizabeth College building to the rear which had endured "patients crowded in rooms, wards, hallways and even the basement." The staff said they treated more Baptists than Presbyterians. Architect H. Eldridge Hannaford of Cincinnati designed the new seven-story hospital of red brick trimmed in stone, doubling the former capacity to 200 beds. The old college building served as overflow rooms or nurses' residence. Hannaford stated that the hospital site was the finest he had ever seen. In 1957 and 1958, two wings were added to this 1940 building. Expansion continues.*

GOOD SAMARITAN HOSPITAL FOR COLORED PEOPLE, CHARLOTTE, N. C.

Charlotte, N. C., Charlotte Sanatorium.

Here's to the Land of the Long Leaf Pine:
The Summer Land, where the sun doth shine:
Where the weak grow strong, and the strong grow great —
Here's to "Down Home", the Old North State!

Good Samaritan Hospital. *A thriving African American neighborhood in Third Ward was anchored at 411 West Hill Street by this twenty-room private hospital for blacks built in 1891. It is said to be the first privately funded, independent hospital in North Carolina built exclusively for the treatment of black patients. It was erected through energetic fund-raising efforts of Charlotte women, primarily Jane Smedburg Wilkes and women of St. Peter's Episcopal Church. Additions in 1925 and 1937 created a 100-bed facility. The hospital sat just west of an Episcopal mission chapel for blacks, St. Michael and All Angels Church. Rooms in the two-story building had hot and cold water and iron cots with springs. In 1959, Memorial Hospital took over "Good Sam," as it was called, continuing operations here as Charlotte Community Hospital. Before the early 1960s, it was the only local hospital where black physicians were allowed to practice in Mecklenburg County. In the 1980s, it became Magnolias Rest Home. The building was razed in 1990 to make room for Ericsson Stadium. (Courtesy Lew Powell)*

Charlotte Sanatorium. *With several small hospitals in the growing uptown area, a group of about thirty leading physicians and surgeons in 1907 organized a private, for-profit sanatorium which a book on Charlotte medical history reports "enjoyed a splendid reputation" and closed in 1942. D. A. Tompkins, who knew how to get things going, was its first president. Architect Frank Milburn designed the three-and-a-half story brick building at 127 West Seventh Street (southeast corner at North Church Street) as a modern general hospital for whites. It had sun parlors, two operating rooms, special hydrotherapeutic equipment, and a training school of forty nurses. Additions by 1929 gave it a 100-room capacity. Subsequently the building served during World War II as the Camp Sutton Station Hospital, Charlotte Sub Station, in 1943. (Camp Sutton, in nearby Monroe, was named for pilot Frank Sutton, the first Union County soldier to die in that war.) In 1944–45 the building was used as a North Carolina State Board of Health clinic. During the years 1947–51, it became the regional office of the U.S. Veterans Administration. The site had in the late 1800s held a home which locals called the Crystal Palace. Discovery Place now occupies the site.*

Mercy Hospital, Charlotte, N. C.—7

Mercy Hospital. *This postcard circa 1935 shows the third home of the hospital founded in 1906 by the Catholic Sisters of Mercy of Belmont, North Carolina. The first building had twenty-five beds in a frame, two-story former parish hall located behind St. Peter's Catholic Church on East First Street. Two sisters at the Belmont convent are credited as the hospital's founders. This postcard's modern, fireproof hospital building on the corner of Caswell Road and 2000 East Fifth Street was surrounded by homes and neat lawns. A four-story addition in 1939 by architects Hook and Hook added beds, an emergency room, and a prenatal clinic and was followed by other additions. The first Negro patient was admitted in 1954. By 1959, thirty beds were assigned for Negro patients. In 1995, the Sisters of Mercy, based in Belmont, sold the hospital to the Charlotte Mecklenburg Hospital Authority, which has continued it as Mercy Hospital with involvement of the Sisters of Mercy.*

TRYON STREET, CHARLOTTE, N. C.

1—CHARLOTTE MEMORIAL HOSPITAL, CHARLOTTE, N. C.

First National Bank and Eye, Ear, Nose and Throat Hospital.
Above the daily first-floor transactions of the First National Bank at 18 South Tryon Street, Dr. Albert M. Whisnant performed surgery and treated patients in his private hospital which occupied the entire third floor. His hospital opened in 1905 (in the wide Italianate building pictured left of center), *but Dr. Whisnant began practice in Charlotte in 1901. A graduate of the Physicians and Surgeons College of Baltimore, Dr. Whisnant also served on the faculty of the North Carolina Medical College (see Schools) and the staff of Charlotte Sanatorium. In 1909, he moved his office to the brand-new high-rise Realty Building (right of center), later called the Independence Building. First National was one of three banks in operation in Charlotte as early as 1867. The bank building was demolished in 1927. The subsequent and continuing hospital called Charlotte Eye, Ear, Nose and Throat Hospital founded in 1918 by Dr. J. P. Matheson and Dr. C. N. Peeler was a specialty hospital, which opened a four-story enterprise in 1923 at 106 West Seventh Street. It was one of the first of its kind in the South. (Postmark 1918).*

Charlotte Memorial Hospital. *This postcard (postmarked 1943) shows the new, public Charlotte Memorial Hospital, which opened in 1940, consolidating with its uptown predecessor, St. Peter's Hospital. Memorial was designed by architect Walter W. Hook on a site at 1000 Blythe Boulevard, between Dilworth Road and East Morehead Street, which was donated by St. Peter's Hospital. Almost immediately, expansion was needed for the original 300-bed structure, and many multistory additions were made over the decades. Additions in the 1960s by A. G. Odell Associates increased the beds to 830. In 1991, the Rush L. Dickson tower greatly expanded and reoriented the building. It was designed by H.K.S. of Dallas. In 1990, the hospital was renamed Carolinas Medical Center.*

Independence Square looking East on Trade St., Charlotte, N. C.—22

Traffic Semaphore. *In the days of horsedrawn wagons, trolleys, and the first autos, a police officer directed traffic during certain hours at the Square. But automobiles' popularity brought traffic problems to the intersection of Trade and Tryon Streets, so in the early 1920s, Police Chief W. B. Orr installed a semaphore, a manually operated stop-and-go sign, the first attempt at traffic control by mechanical means. It stood on an iron base in the center of the crossroads, and later a signal light was operated electrically by a patrolman in a tower on the southwest corner of Independence Square. When cars approached, he changed the sign. The system was subsequently extended a block each way from the Square on Trade and Tryon Streets. Around 1918, four policemen were assigned to patrol on bicycles. Postmarked 1923.*

Burwell-Walker Company. *At 211 South Church Street, Chalmers motor cars were sold to Charlotteans eager to drive about town and into the countryside on Sunday afternoons, scaring horses and rural folks with their newfangled autos. Burwell-Walker Co. was an automobile distributor with Armistead Burwell, president (1917), and J. O. Walker, vice-president, selling Dort, Chalmers, and Oldsmobiles through 1921. The firm later became Burwell-Harris Co., auto sales and garage at 227–233 North Tryon Street. (Courtesy Lake County Museum Illinois, Curt Teich Postcard Archives)*

BURWELL-WALKER CO., CHARLOTTE, N. C.

New Bridge at Rozzelle's Ferry. *Ever since the band of federal troops called "Stoneman's Raiders" burned the key bridge over the Catawba River at Rozzelle's Ferry in 1865, citizens and especially Charlotte merchants clamored for a new bridge to Lincoln and Gaston Counties. Finally, in 1910, this shining, four-span steel bridge, 612 feet long and 16 feet wide, opened. Built on rock piers from the old Civil War–era bridge at a cost of $15,000, it rose 28 feet above low-water level, higher than the old span, "thus ensuring safety against floods." But in the great flood of 1916, all bridges across the Catawba between Charlotte and Asheville were swept away with riverbank cotton mills, homes, cattle, and barns. Eighty people died in this disaster.*

New Bridge at Rozzelle's Ferry, on Road to Charlotte, N. C.

Charlotte, N. C.,
View of Interurban Depot.

Charlotte, N. C.,
View of Catawba River Along Interurban.

Interurban Depot on Mint Street. *You are looking at a popular idea! From 1911, when textile mills dotted riverbanks along the rocky, wide Catawba River, many millworkers, farmers and other folk needed to get to Charlotte to shop or work or to be entertained at Lakewood Park, for example. Few owned cars, and trains didn't go west of Charlotte along the textile corridor. The idea of an interurban electric line connecting textile mill towns between Gastonia and Charlotte became a splendid venture by tobacco tycoon James B. Duke and engineer W. S. Lee as part of Duke's string of hydro dams to harness water power and develop industry in the Piedmont Carolinas. Architects Hook and Rogers got the contract for depots to "dot this great trolley system." The Gastonia-Charlotte line began in 1912, connecting the streetcar systems of both towns and through Belmont, Mount Holly, Cramerton, etc. First called the Interurban, and later the Piedmont and Northern (1911), it stopped at depots like this one pictured in Charlotte. This view of the Catawba is a typical scene from the Interurban's windows before the manmade lakes named Mountain Island, Wylie, and Norman changed the vista. The Catawba's original character, with severe seasonal rising and falling, had kept it a historically nonnavigable river above Great Falls, South Carolina, near the state line. The arrival of rail transportation to mill towns along the Catawba was extremely welcome. P&N passenger service ended in 1951. Seaboard Coast Line bought controlling interest in the P&N freight service in 1968.*

Mecklenburg Road and their Builders,
Charlotte, N. C.

Mecklenburg County Roads and Their Builders. *Strangling mud and axle-deep ruts led officials to push for better roads "to lift Charlotte out of the mud" in the 1880s-1910s. The invention of the motorcar and increased manufacturing and farm production made compelling reasons. In 1888, prison labor was first authorized by the state legislature specifically for Mecklenburg County. In 1899, farmers were paid forty cents per cubic yard for loose native rock delivered to collection sites. In 1907, the cost of feeding, clothing, and guarding a convict working on the road was twenty-five cents a day. By 1909, the county boasted of several belt roads, including 200 miles of macadamized roads, which were drained roadbeds covered with three graduated layers of rock, starting with coarse, large rocks on the bottom. Two forces of convict labor constantly crushed rock, scraped, rolled, and spread surfaces. The convict camps moved three or four times a year and in summer used pitched tents within two to four miles of the worksite. The handwritten message on the back of this card dated 1912 reads, "What good roads there are here are made [sic] by this system." Convict road crews (pictured in lower view) wore distinctive striped uniforms. When chained together, they were called a chain gang.*

Southern R.R. Depot, Charlotte, N.C.

Southern Rail Road Depot. *Southern Railway, second station, built in 1905, on West Trade Street was designed by Frank Milburn. This Spanish mission–style train station with its red-tile roof and mock campanile replaced the old station on the same site which had earlier been the Richmond and Danville passenger station. In 1888, the city had four train depots for the heavy passenger and freight cars which passed through town. When this depot opened, crowds wandered through the*

flower-filled waiting room testing the shiny new cuspidors and admiring the fancy details. Until 1914, Gresham's Southern Railway Dining Room was located here. Customers could buy quail on toast for a nickel a plate. Travelers had trouble, however, with the muddy streets and infrequency of "hacks" (horse-drawn carriages) for transportation. This station was the starting point for parades and was close to the best hotels in town. It was razed in 1963.

Bus Station. *The Union Bus Station, built at 418 West Trade Street and designed by architect J. A. Malcolm, shows the sleek, curving glass brick that wraps around corners and the unornamented tile front of the era's Art Moderne style. L. A. Love, president of the Queen City Coach Co., announced plans for this "new, modern, and comfortable bus terminal" in 1940. It replaced an outdated station next door at 410 West Trade Street. The two-story, air-conditioned facility was reported in the Charlotte Observer to have white and Negro waiting rooms, each with its own cafe or restaurant concession. Men's rooms with showers were downstairs, and a ladies' room with mirrors, dressing tables, and showers were upstairs, along with offices. It later became the Trailways station, which closed this terminal and moved to the Greyhound station at 601 West Trade Street in 1987. The Union Bus Station was converted into a business office.*

Municipal Airport. *Several informal landing fields of "doubtful safety" preceded the city airport's official opening in 1937. A joint effort of Charlotte bonds and the Works Progress Administration created 1) unemployment relief during the Great Depression and 2) an airport for Charlotte with three runways for air mail and passenger service by Eastern Air Lines. To honor his visionary efforts, the airport was officially named Douglas Municipal Airport for Mayor Ben Douglas in 1940. A U.S. Commerce official had recommended the location near the Southern rail line and a dual-lane highway (Wilkinson Boulevard), since early pilots flew by the "iron compass" (railroad tracks) to guide them in. In 1912, Charlotte's Thornwell Andrews flew his Curtiss biplane for about twenty-three minutes at the May 20 "Meck Dec" celebration, the first flight over Charlotte. The hangar pictured, built in 1936–37 by the WPA, remains in use as the Carolinas Aviation Museum at 4108 Airport Drive. The terminal building was torn down about 1968.*

Johnny Crowell. *Johnny Crowell was Charlotte's best-known aviator, described on this postcard as the "Worlds Champion Hands Off Pilot." With his hands tied, the daredevil flew in an air show on September 7, 1947. He set world records with his single-engine plane when he flew four outside loops in a minute. Crowell is credited with obtaining public support for building a Charlotte airport. He became the first airport manager. His inventions led to improvements in aerial photography and compasses for cross-country flying. Often assisting in local news stories, he flew* Charlotte News *staff writer Dorothy Knox over the city in April 1936 to assess flood damage. Among the disasters they witnessed was the broken dam that flooded Lakewood Amusement Park.*

Carolina Central Freight Depot. *Looking eastward downhill on Trade Street toward the edge of town, note the Carolina Freight Depot (streetside center, right), a two-story red brick building, with five windows on its second floor, a gray hipped roof and cupola, and a long, low one-story wing extending right for loading cotton and other freight. The rail line paralleled the far side of the building, crossing East Trade Street, and was part of the track that first brought celebrated rail service to Charlotte in 1852. The Carolina Central Railway Co. was in operation in Charlotte in 1861. It had a separate passenger depot at Tryon and Thirteenth Streets by 1874. Folks could ship goods or ride to North Carolina places like Shoe Heel, Moss Banks, Red Banks, Matthews, Hamlet, and Wilmington to the east, or west to Buffalo, Lincolnton, or Shelby. In the 1890s, the Carolina Central became part of the Seaboard Air Line Railroad.*

Primary and Preparatory School

Charlotte Kindergarten, Charlotte, N. C.

Charlotte Kindergarten. *In the first half of the twentieth century and certainly in the century preceding, public kindergartens were unknown. Private homes were often used as kindergartens for small children, and many of these were located in a teacher's residence. The pleasing, early-twentieth-century house on this postcard was one. There were several kindergartens on Elizabeth Avenue, one offering private tutoring, others with a private school following kindergarten.*

CHARLOTTE, N. C.   Charlotte Public Schools   5083

The Daniel Harvey Hill School *at the corner of South Boulevard and East Morehead Streets was long known as South Graded School for first grade to graduates in the tenth grade. A resident recalled, "All the children in the city went to that school. In 1897 and for some years after, bicycles were in general use, especially by school girls and boys, and it was a show to see those older boys and girls, come out of school in the afternoon, form in a parade about eight cycles wide and more than that many deep and come abreast up South Tryon Street, the parade growing smaller as one after another fell out at home or on to a side street."*

Initially the D. H. Hill School was built in 1859 as the North Carolina Military Institute. It was the creation of Davidson College math professor D. H. Hill in preparation for a civil war he felt was clearly imminent. The building was modeled after his alma mater, the U.S. Military Academy at West Point. It served as a training school for cadets, then for Confederate troops. In a large washhouse on the school grounds, Charlotte ladies established a hospital for soldiers passing through town. (Later on, the Confederate government took charge of the Wayside Hospital and used the buildings of the Carolina Fair Association near Morehead Street. At the close of the war, the "Old Red House" on Trade Street was used as a hospital.)

In 1883, the building pictured reopened as the city's white school and the city's first tax-supported public graded school. It later became an elementary school. The building was used for school maintenance supplies in the early 1950s and was razed in 1954.

HORNER MILITARY SCHOOL, CHARLOTTE, N. C.

CENTRAL HIGH SCHOOL, CHARLOTTE, N. C.

Horner Military School. *On the outer edge of the Myers Park neighborhood which opened in 1912, young men paraded in formation at the Horner Military School campus near Selwyn Avenue in 1914. Founded in central North Carolina in 1851, the school moved from Hillsborough and later Oxford, where its buildings burned. Colonel Jerome C. Horner, son of the founder, brought to Myers Park its solid reputation for discipline, the classics, and "no compromise with irregularity." The completed streetcar line ended near Horner, which closed in 1920 when fifty acres belonging to the school were sold. Some of the buildings were used for the early Myers Park Country Club, and one was later adapted for condominiums at 2501 Roswell Avenue.*

Central High School. *Charlotte was growing to such an extent around 1920 that the North School and the South School were insufficient for white students. In 1922, this three-story Central High School was built, but not without controversy, because its 5.3-acre site was low-lying, overgrown land beside Sugar Creek, a large prone-to-flooding stream which crosses beneath Elizabeth Avenue. Builders spent about $11,000 driving pilings for foundations of the school designed by architects Lockwood, Green and Co. Estimated total construction cost was $242,000. After World War II, returning GIs attended night classes here in a program which became Charlotte College through the efforts of Dr. Bonnie Cone, later expanding onto another campus to become UNC-Charlotte. This building at 1141 Elizabeth Avenue became part of the campus of Central Piedmont Community College. High on the upper left facade, the original terrazzo motto reads "Knowledge Is Power."*

North School (*First Ward Graded School at East Ninth and North Brevard Streets*). *This odd-looking building was the pride of Charlotte in 1900 when it opened as a white public school for students in the northern half of town. Soon it became local custom to ring this school's bell first on New Year's Eve at midnight as a signal for every other bell and steam whistle in town to join in the bedlam. Townsfolk rushed from their houses to listen. Earlier, the bell rang loud and long from the belfry in the rear of the old courthouse on West Trade Street.*

The school's design was chosen when the school superintendent studied sample plans by architect Frank Milburn of Washington, D.C. He liked best a Texas hospital plan with wings radiating from a central core and bay windows in each of the eighteen classrooms. Constructed for $27,000, it also had a large basement play-room for physical activities on rainy days. A big to-do was made over the cornerstone containing archives to edify the future, such as the Bible, the state flag, a copy of the Mecklenburg Declaration of Independence, photos of living Confederate veterans, drawings, seeds, a May 20 centennial coin, a North Carolina military button, a booklet about the city in 1900, and a poem. In 1904, North School had 981 students and 18 teachers. The two other public schools in town were the South School in the old Carolina Military Institute building (1,003 pupils), and the Myers Street School for blacks (1,111 pupils). North School was demolished in the 1970s.

Charlotte, N. C., The Industrial Center of the New South, First Ward Graded School.

Biddle Institute/Johnson C. Smith University.

With the close of the Civil War in 1865, African Americans were finally free to form schools and churches. In 1867, several white Northern Presbyterian ministers got a charter for a school to educate southern black ministers and teachers, funded by $10,000 from the Freedmen's Bureau and $1,900 from Philadelphian Mary Biddle, whose Union soldier husband had been killed at Gettysburg. Organizers who met in a small church at Fourth and Davidson Streets bought lumber salvaged from the Charlotte Confederate Navy Yard to build the school. William R. Myers gave eight acres on a hilltop west of town at 100 Beatties Ford Road for the school which was named Henry J. Biddle Memorial Institute.

Administration Building, Biddle University, Charlotte, N. C.

Biddle Hall.

Five-story Biddle Hall, pictured with its Victorian clocktower constructed in 1883–84, is on the National Register of Historic Places. It became a Charlotte-Mecklenburg Historic Landmark in 1976. The early buildings pictured were a lonely group of isolated college structures but became the center of a strong black neighborhood known as Biddle Heights, reached by streetcar in 1903. In 1923, the school's name changed to Johnson C. Smith University, with over $700,000 donated by the widow of Smith, a Pittsburgh druggist. The school expanded its acreage and educated black Presbyterian ministers, doctors, dentists, and teachers. The Duke Endowment's 1980s grant of $500,000 handsomely restored the leaking, aging Biddle Hall.

PRESBYTERIAN COLLEGE
CHARLOTTE, N.C.

Elizabeth College, Charlotte, N. C.

Presbyterian College. *Riding on the streetcar from the Square, riders turned onto the street pictured (the one-block-long College Avenue, later named Phifer Avenue) and approached the college which filled the entire block of North College Street between Ninth and Tenth Streets. Presbyterian Female College (chartered 1896) built this imposing institution in 1900–1901 and renamed it Presbyterian College for Women in 1910. Nicholas Ittner was the builder. The three-story school had a large entry rotunda, a formal parlor, dormitories, dining room for 250, gym, and an auditorium seating about 1,000. But the college stayed here only thirteen years. Renamed Queens College, it moved in 1914 to a campus and five new buildings in brand-new Myers Park, enticed by fifty free acres of land and infrastructure, with some of the donated acreage to be sold for endowment funds. This building pictured was to have become a high school, but instead it was remodeled by C. C. Hook and the Stephens Co. in 1919 for the College Apartments. Its auditorium was used quite happily by the Little Theater in the 1930s, except when trains roared by during performances. It was razed in 1948.*

Elizabeth College. *Lutheran pastor Charles D. King had a dream. He wanted to offer young southern women an education in "classics, mathematics and sciences equal to . . . our best colleges for young men" and to add training in "social culture, music, art and conversation." The first brick buildings of Elizabeth College were built in 1896–97 on the former Charles Law Torrence plantation at the end of a leisurely lane just beyond the eastern edge of Charlotte, when the town population was about 18,000. The Reverend King named the small Victorian college for Anne Elizabeth Watts, whose husband's tobacco fortune largely financed the college. People from all over Charlotte came to musical events and plays at the college conservatory. A formal entry gate and a thick, thorny hedge of locust was "planted all around the college, to keep the girls in and the boys out." Beyond the college lay fields where townspeople found fine rabbit, squirrel, and bird hunting in days when citizens commonly ate all three. The central college building, designed by architect J. A. Dempwolf of Pennsylvania, later became Presbyterian Hospital. Elizabeth College moved to Salem, Virginia, in 1915.*

13400—Road from Elizabeth College to Charlotte, N. C.

Road from Elizabeth College. *Imagine standing in the spacious front yard of Elizabeth College in the early 1900s. Look toward uptown, where the ridgeline is visible far in the distance. In front of you is Elizabeth Avenue, beginning at the college entrance and stretching toward uptown along an avenue of oaks, telephone poles, and large frame homes. It is thoroughly residential as it merges into East Trade Street until you get within several uphill blocks of the Square. Beyond the street median (center) is the trolley. Everyone rode streetcars in the Charlotte trolley era of 1891–1938: businessmen, children, servants, students, soldiers, shoppers, and mill workers.*

QUEENS COLLEGE, CHARLOTTE, N. C.

Queens College. *Five handsome brick buildings with red-tiled roofs and trimmed in Indiana limestone were completed in the Myers Park neighborhood in time for the fall 1914 semester. They are still used by the college. Architect C. C. Hook of Charlotte designed the buildings for the newly renamed women's college which moved to the new campus. In town it had been named Presbyterian College for Women (chartered in 1896; see page 136), and in earlier days called Charlotte Female Academy (founded 1857) at Ninth and College Streets. Soon after Queens' opening in Myers Park, students rode the new streetcar line which was extended to Queens from uptown Charlotte.*

Second Ward School, (For Colored), Charlotte, N. C.—40

ADMINISTRATION BUILDING, THOMPSON ORPHANAGE
CHARLOTTE, N. C.

Second Ward School. *When this school, the first public high school for blacks in Mecklenburg County, was built in 1923, it was a source of great pride to school officials and the African American community. It was not only a first, it was also part of a program to replace wooden schools with new brick ones. Prior to Second Ward School, schools for blacks offered classes to students only as far as the ninth or tenth grades. This school had classroom laboratories, a library, auditorium, domestic science and domestic art departments, and a manual training shop. After World War II, the school facility doubled as a daytime high school and a two-year college (Carver College) in late afternoons and evenings. Carver later became part of Central Piedmont Community College. The building was demolished in 1969 and the Metro School was built on the site at 700 East Second Street.*

Thompson Orphanage. *Small children of Thompson Orphanage pose in front of the red-brick, 1920s Bronson Memorial Hall used for classrooms and later the Administration Building. It was named for the land donor, the Reverend Benjamin Bronson, a transplanted New England schoolteacher and former rector of St. Peter's Episcopal Church, which first sponsored the home and training institution. It had begun in 1886 to aid the many destitute families and homeless children in decades following the Civil War. Bertie County's wealthy Lewis Thompson, for whom the orphanage was named, gave funds for the facility. Bricks for early buildings were made from nearby creek-bank clay. The orphanage eventually included a row of brick cottages, a chapel, and a large working farm and dairy on land along Sugar Creek between what later became Midtown Square and Central Piedmont Community College. The chapel at Kings Drive and Third Street, owned by the city, is all that remains of the campus.*

Charlotte, N.C. North Carolina Medical College.

North Carolina Medical College. *The artist who hand-colored this card painted out the well-known Old Settlers' Cemetery (green space at left), perhaps because its presence so near the brick North Carolina Medical College presented a disturbing view. Four hospitals and a sanatorium surrounded the uptown location at 229 North Church at Sixth Street. It was the only medical school for whites in the state when this building was erected in 1907. Architect J. M. McMichael designed the three-story structure specifically for medical treatment and teaching. A two-story amphitheater enabled about 250 students to watch surgical proceedings beneath the wall-etched motto in German: "I Serve." Cadaver vats were in use in the basement. The medical school had been started in 1887 by Dr. Paul Barringer, who sold it to Dr. John Peter Munroe in 1889. Patients for a free clinic from 11:00 to noon weekdays sat in separate waiting rooms for whites and blacks. Treatment rooms, dissecting and lecture halls, laboratories, library, reading room, and offices were the pride of "the bald-headed bachelor father of NCMC," Davidson College physician Dr. J. P. Munroe. It had no official connection with Davidson College and subsequently moved to Charlotte, chartered as the North Carolina Medical College in 1893, a three-year institution. In 1907, it had eighty-two full-time students. Doctor of Medicine degrees were awarded to 340 physicians during its lifetime, 1887–1914. The College then merged with the Medical College of Virginia. The important building later became apartments, the Pickler Hotel, and offices. The building became a Charlotte-Mecklenburg Historic Landmark in 1979. Settlers' Cemetery became a Charlotte-Mecklenburg Historic Landmark in 1984 and was restored in 1998.*

Davidson, N.C., Martin Chemical Laboratory, Davidson College.

"O'Donoghue Hall", Charlotte, N. C.

Martin Chemical Laboratory, Davidson College, Davidson, N.C.

At commencement in 1896, the Reverend Charles G. Vardell (class of 1888) discarded his prepared speech and spoke to alumni about Davidson College's serious need for a science building. Members of the college pledged several thousand dollars immediately. This chemistry building became a tribute to Colonel W. J. Martin, a well-known college science professor who, according to Dr. Paul Barringer of the Medical College of Virginia, had for a generation been "making chemists, without a laboratory, by the unique process of making men first, that could become chemists or anything else they undertook." The building which stood during years 1901–41, was the ninth campus building at Davidson College, a liberal arts college founded by Presbyterians in 1837 for men. This handsome brick, two-story building designed by Hook and Sawyer held classrooms, offices, stockrooms, and three large laboratories.

O'Donoghue Hall. *Built in 1905 at 531 South Tryon Street, this building had a Catholic beginning and an Elks Club ending. Founded at another location by the Sisters of Mercy in 1887, the Catholic school was first named St. Mary's Seminary. When it moved to this new building at the northeast corner of Stonewall and South Tryon Streets, it became O'Donoghue Hall, named for Charlotte benefactor and physician Dr. Dennis O'Donoghue. Dr. O'Donoghue was a native of Ireland who emigrated in 1871 and completed his training in the United States. Within this same city block in the early 1900s was O'Donoghue Hall, the Sisters of Mercy convent, the fledgling Mercy Hospital, and St. Peter's Catholic Church. In 1931, O'Donoghue Hall stood vacant, but soon it became the Salvation Army Family and Transient Bureau (1932–36), Geyer Business College (1938–43), Service Men's Quarters (1944), and the Elks Club (about 1945). A huge elk's head loomed over the entry with a sign that read "B.P.O.E." (Benevolent and Protective Order of Elks). The building burned in 1948, was rebuilt as a new Elks Club in 1951, and was razed in 1997.*

11. Soldiers and Heroes *Military, Parades, and Monuments*

Notable Guests, May 20, 1909.
Pres. Taft, Gov. Kitchin, Mrs. Stonewall Jackson at Charlotte, N. C.

Notable Guests, May 20, 1909. *Portly U.S. president William Howard Taft is flanked by Governor William W. Kitchin (to Taft's left), and Mrs. Stonewall Jackson, at Taft's right. The petite Mrs. Jackson, 77, often dressed in black silk. Note Taft's top hat resting on the lower shelf of the table, the ornate silver water pitcher, and two oriental rugs spread beneath them at the front of the temporary grandstand built for the occasion. The sloping 3,000-seat grandstand encircled the trees (back right)*

which were on the lawn of the 301 South Tryon Street courthouse where Taft was due to speak. But suddenly rain came in torrents, and the speeches and notables fled several blocks to the dry, drafty City Auditorium at College and Fifth Streets. People who hung red bunting on their houses said it bled mightily in the rain, leaving vivid, red-stained memories of the occasion.

The City in Holiday Dress. *Charlotte's recipe for celebrating Mecklenburg Declaration of Independence Day annually was to drape the Square, streets, and buildings. Looking across the Square (left), the banner reads "20th of May Celebration" and notes festivities of May 21–26. The tall City Hall spire punctuates the background on North Tryon Street, and the four-story Central Hotel (right) on the Square at South Tryon Street goes all out. Postmarked 1910.*

E 9308 CHARLOTTE, N.C. THE INDUSTRIAL CENTRE OF THE NEW SOUTH
THE CITY IN HOLIDAY DRESS, LOOKING UP TRYON STREET TOWARD CITY HALL.

PLATE COMMEMORATING THE SIGNING OF THE MECKLENBURG DECLARATION OF INDEPENDENCE.

MECKLENBURG DECLARATION
OF
INDEPENDENCE.
MAY 20, 1775.
DEFENCE OF
CHARLOTTE.
SEPT. 26.
1780.

CENTER OF PUBLIC SQUARE, CHARLOTTE, N. C.

Mecklenburg Declaration of Independence Street Marker. *It was dangerous to look for it, better to view it by postcard, this handsome middle-of-the-crossroads plaque at the Square. It commemorates the Mecklenburg Declaration of Independence of 1775.*

Signed by early Mecklenburg leaders, the document declared the county independent of British government more than a year prior to the American Declaration of Independence on July 4, 1776. The marker also notes the revolutionary Battle of Charlotte in 1780 against British troops. In the 1890s, this plaque noted the historic events, but incessant traffic wore it thin. In 1947, a new one was cast at the insistence of Julia Alexander, lawyer and descendant of a signer of the 1775 document.

Twentieth of May in Charlotte
One of the Entrances to Court of Honor

Twentieth of May, Entrance to Court of Honor. *Whenever possible, Charlotte staged special occasions on May 20, and 1909 was no exception. President William Howard Taft came to town for the final day of a three-day celebration of Mecklenburg Declaration of Independence Day. This May 20 arch was located on West Trade Street. Identical arches spanned North and South Tryon Streets, together accenting three main arteries approaching the Square. Streetcars used the large center opening and wagons or autos used the two small arched openings. Electricity was still a great novelty, and the lights strung to the right and left were part of the 1,800 lights for the event. Five thousand small flags decorated the grandstand where tickets were sold for a view of the parade and festivities. Citizens went wild with decoration fever, hanging 425 large flags and 2,500 yards of bunting on mercantile buildings, beginning with the Charlotte Daily Observer Building which was draped on all four floors. Bands played at the Square where seventy twenty-foot white columns lined the streets between the arches and the Square, heralding the Court of Honor. For visitors and locals, three carnivals gave daily performances. Taft was royally entertained during his twelve-hour train stopover, in particular at the Selwyn Hotel where razorback hog was served in the private dining room. The room was decorated in green and white, the colors of Yale, Taft's alma mater. Charlotte wanted visitors to note the new incandescent streetlights and cement sidewalks, but Taft noticed the live possum chained to the top of a fire engine. After all, Taft's political nickname was "Possum Billy."*

Parade Car. *Young Elizabeth Miller, daughter of Mr. and Mrs. R. M. Miller Jr., sits behind her driver in the back of the Miller auto decorated for the annual May 20 parade celebrating the Mecklenburg Declaration of Independence, 1775. Note the hornets' nests in tree branches sprouting from the windshield as symbols of local patriots' rebellion. Flags of North Carolina bear the May 20th date and drape the car. Even the tires wear patriotic colors. The car waits in the porte cochere of the imposing Miller residence at 406 North Tryon Street. (See Residences). A note written by Arabelle Johnson on the back of the postcard declares this is "the first gasoline automobile I ever rode in."*

CHARLOTTE. N.C.
THE
INDUSTRIAL CENTER
OF THE NEW SOUTH.

MONUMENT TO THE SIGNERS OF THE FIRST
AMERICAN DECLARATION OF INDEPENDENCE
MAY 20TH 1775

STONE &
BARRINGER C.
PUBLISHERS

HAND-COLORED.

Monument to Signers. *In 1842, local folks began to raise money for a monument honoring the men who signed the Mecklenburg Declaration of Independence on May 20, 1775. But the Civil War intervened, and later a bank failure lost $5,000 they had collected. Citizens resumed the campaign and finally a procession and unveiling of the granite and bronze obelisk were held early in the morning of May 20, 1898. A mile-long parade started on South Tryon Street with horsemen, carriages, floats, and Confederate veterans. Mrs. Stonewall Jackson was in the place of honor. At the courthouse grounds on 301 South Tryon Street where the obelisk stood, eight young girls, all descendants of Signers, wore white organdy dresses with colored sashes. They pulled the ropes to reveal the monument crafted by Gualt of Baltimore. Earlier, crowds heard a speech by the Honorable Adlai Ewing Stevenson of Illinois, former U.S. vice president, who spoke at a platform in the First Presbyterian churchyard. Onlookers on that sunny day reported the "great celebration . . . went merry as a marriage bell." The monument was later moved to 700 East Trade Street in front of the fifth Mecklenburg County Courthouse.*

1847-1907
BRONZE BUST OF JOHN CHARLES McNEIL,
Unveiled Oct. 17th, 1914. Presented by Woman's Club of Charlotte to the City,
North Carolina's best loved poet.
Author of Songs, Merry and Sad, and Lyrics from Cotton Land.

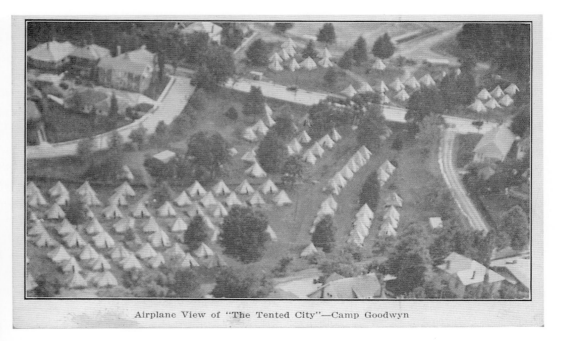

Airplane View of "The Tented City"—Camp Goodwyn

Camp Goodwyn. *The 300-tent area was called Camp Goodwyn, named for General A. T. Goodwyn. It was set up to provide temporary quarters for a huge overflowing crowd which attended the 39th Reunion of the United Confederate Veterans of 1929. The location was near Kings Drive and Elizabeth Avenue.*

left

Bronze Bust of John Charles McNeill. *Poet, journalist, lawyer, and fisherman, McNeill was best known for his writing in the* Charlotte Observer, *where he was "an irregular member of the staff," on the payroll but without deadlines. His accounts of "little loves and sorrows" took the form of poems, reviews, reportage of murders, the Baptist State Convention, or the inauguration of Theodore Roosevelt. Two books contain his folksy, lyrical poems which were widely memorized and quoted and led to his being named the poet laureate of North Carolina. He lived upstairs at the Southern Manufacturers' Club, often watching street events from the roof garden, but he preferred streams and fields like those in his native Scotland County, where he was born in 1874 (not the date given on the postcard). In his law office in Laurinburg, he kept a pet possum. Skinny and tall, McNeill had a booming voice which one newspaperman wrote "sounds like a pipe organ would if somebody played its bass notes in the great caves of Kentucky." The McNeill bust is located in the Robinson-Spangler Carolina Room at the Public Library of Charlotte-Mecklenburg County. Postcards consistently misspell McNeill's name.*

CONFEDERATE MONUMENT IN ELMWOOD CEMETERY
ERECTED IN 1887 BY LADIES MEMORIAL ASSOCIATION

Confederate Monument in Elmwood Cemetery. *Unlike many southern towns, Charlotte never erected the familiar statue of a Confederate soldier in the courthouse square. Instead, this granite obelisk was raised in the city cemetery, Elmwood, at 700 West Sixth Street which was then on the edge of town in 1887, twenty-two years after the Civil War's end. Newspaper accounts describe schoolchildren on Confederate Memorial Day May 10th, parading from the Square carrying a garland of flowers to decorate the monument as shown in this postcard. Mrs. Stonewall Jackson, a Charlotte native and widow of the Confederate general, usually led the parade. The marker reads: "Erected by the Women of Charlotte, to the Confederate Soldiers of Mecklenburg County and The Unknown Soldiers who rest here. 1861–1865. We Honor Them and Revere Them." In 1870, the Memorial Association raised funds to have the bodies of one hundred and sixty nine soldiers moved from a field near the Wayside Hospital and the Rudisill Gold Mine to Elmwood Cemetery. Jonas Rudisill made the coffins and kept the name and death date of each soldier. The Confederate holiday was scheduled differently by various southern states. North Carolina chose May 10th in honor of the death of Stonewall Jackson.*

Auditorium—Camp Goodwyn while work is going on—May 31, '29

SITE OF CONFEDERATE STATES NAVY YARD.
OPERATED 1862 AND 1865, CHARLOTTE N. C.

Auditorium. *Rushed to completion in 1929, this auditorium at 310 North Kings Drive was finished in seventy-three working days, just in time for use as the central meeting place of the 39th Reunion of United Confederate Veterans. Some veterans were one hundred years old but they came anyway, bringing their families. An estimated 50,000–70,000 soldiers and visitors streamed into Charlotte. In addition to the tent city, more rooms were needed in homes, Thompson Orphanage, Central High, Elizabeth School, St. John's Baptist Church, and Queens College. The veterans enjoyed commissary meals at the auditorium, and programs including Marine Band music, a boxing match, a historical pageant, and a grand finale parade of 10,000 veterans of three wars marching through town with 150,000 citizens lining the streets. Most popular were the horse show at the Polo Grounds and a ball at the auditorium. The building designed by architect Marion R. Marsh replaced the Charlotte Auditorium at Fifth and College Streets. The auditorium pictured burned in 1954. Park Center was built on the site, reusing some of the foundation walls, and it was later renamed Grady Cole Center.*

Confederate Navy Yard. *Modern buildings occupying the site of the Confederate Navy Yard (1862–65) have successively worn this ornate marker, which was unveiled on June 3, 1910, Jefferson Davis's birthday. It commemorates one of the most interesting eras in Charlotte history. The iron shield, surrounded by sea cables and mounted on anchors, represents the harrowing years of the Civil War, when Gosport Naval Yard in Norfolk, Virginia, was in danger of capture by Union troops. Charlotte, with its railroad, an established iron works, and inland location, was chosen as the site of the new, safer navy yard. Workers came to work in the gun carriage construction shop, the large forge shop, coke ovens, and the foundry where they forged wrought-iron projectiles, torpedoes, and propeller shaftings for Confederate gun boats. The marker, which weighs 85 pounds and cost $25 in 1910, was cast at the J. Frank Wilkes family's company, the Mecklenburg Iron Works. The site is in the 200 block on the south side of East Trade Street at the railroad underpass (former Civic Center site).*

Camp Greene. *Charlotte's sedate southern pace suddenly changed when high-powered local men besieged Washington where they competed with Wilmington, Fayetteville, and Savannah for a World War I army training camp for Charlotte in 1917. Charlotte was chosen. Within months, the town of about 50,000 was turned upside down. Camp Greene was named for a Revolutionary War general, Nathanael Greene from Rhode Island, whose southern victories made him a national hero.*

Doubling the existing town population, more than 60,000 soldiers would arrive to train in trench warfare, cavalry, artillery, and small arms defense. The camp covered 2,600 acres and hired more than 7,500 workers to build a wooden city of 980 buildings, large and small, doubletime in five weeks. A worker recalled, "We built a building an hour!"

Rapidly collected parcels of land had been amassed around the pivotal farm on a high knoll west of Charlotte, the 248-acre James C. Dowd farm. The Dowds' 1880 farmhouse at 2216 Monument Street became temporary camp head-quarters, but the lovely peach, apple, and pear orchards, the grape arbor, and cotton fields were cleared and replaced with a tent city, stables, hospitals, roads, and thousands of khaki-clad men from the Northwest and New England, soon to be sent to French battlefields. In that harsh southern winter of 1918 and its severe influenza epidemic, thousands died in Camp Greene instead. The Dowd house became a Charlotte-Mecklenburg Historic Landmark in 1978.

"THE OLD DOWD HOME" ARMY HEADQUARTERS AT CAMP GREENE, CHARLOTTE, N. C.

U. S. NATIONAL GUARD CANTONMENT, CAMP GREENE, CHARLOTTE, N. C.

VIEW FROM DOWD ROAD SHOWING MESS HALL, TENTS AND WATER TANK NO. 1.

U. S. NATIONAL GUARD CANTONMENT, CAMP GREENE, CHARLOTTE, N. C.

LECTURING ON MILITARY TACTICS.

INTERIOR OF BARRACKS, Camp Greene, Charlotte, N. C.

COMPANY STREET, TENTS AIRING, Camp Greene, Charlotte, N. C.

PIEDMONT CIGAR STORE, COR. TRADE AND CHURCH STREETS, CHARLOTTE, N. C.

Piedmont Cigar Store. *During World War I, when soldiers soon to be shipped out to France were training in 1917–18 at Charlotte's Camp Greene, the Piedmont Cigar Store at 201 West Trade Street was a popular spot. Here army men and uptown businessmen gathered for cigars, pipes, soft drinks, lunch, and smokes. From a timely ad:*

> *Dressed up in their suits of brown,*
> *Our soldier boys hike into town.*
> *The hike is apt to make them think*
> *That the thing they need is a cold drink*
> *Or maybe they'll receive a hunch*
> *That something tells they need lunch,*
> *Or a smoke of the brands they smoked of yore,*
> *So they hike into a Piedmont Store*
> *Where they'll find the best that can be had*
> *To make them satisfied and glad.*

Confederate Window Display. *The most prominent spot for any uptown window display was at the Woodall and Sheppard Drugstore on the corner at the Square. When the reunion of the North Carolina Division of United Confederate Veterans held a reunion on August 26, 1909, this display showed a portrait of General Robert E. Lee, Confederate money, and military relics. After a barbecue at Latta Park, 1,085 of the 2,000 veterans present paraded behind their mounted leaders in a "picturesque spectacle." All traffic stopped for an hour while crowds lined sidewalks from St. Peter's Catholic Church at First Street all the way to Fifth Street on North Tryon Street. The only surviving Confederate drum corps led the parade as the veterans sang "Dixie" marching behind the tattered banners of the war.*

Post Office & Monument to Lieut. William E. Shipp, killed at the Battle of Santiago, Charlotte, N. C.

13418

Spanish Cannon (bottom left in front of post office). *The formidable cannon, which was moved from several public locations around Charlotte, first arrived in 1900 heralded by this newspaper announcement which refers to the Spanish-American War: "The cannon captured by Americans at Santiago and presented to the City of Charlotte by the government through the influence of Senator Pritchard, arrived in Charlotte Sunday night and is being mounted in front of the post office [401 West Trade]." Markings on the cannon indicate it was cast in Barcelona, Spain, in 1769. The mounting was cast at Mecklenburg Iron Works. Young pranksters who attempted to load and fire the cannon in the 1920s were thwarted by an alert security guard. Among them was James Stenhouse, who later became a well-known architect and historian. The cannon now sits at 3500 Shamrock Drive at the Charlotte Museum of History.*

The Shipp Monument (obelisk at right front). *In 1902, four years after the Spanish-American War, Congress approved the petition to erect a monument on federal property in Charlotte to honor the late Lieutenant William Ewen Shipp (1861–98), who died near San Juan, Cuba, in the Battle of Santiago. Lieutenant Shipp lived in Charlotte, attended the Carolina Military Institute, and in 1883 was the first southerner graduated from West Point after the Civil War. Schoolchildren throughout North Carolina donated funds to pay for the fifteen-ton, thirty-foot shaft of Winnsboro granite. The monument today is located at the corner of Fourth and Mint Streets behind the Jonas Federal building. During construction projects, it has been moved to different sites on the federal property.*

Ex-President J. K. Polk Monument, Fort Mill, S. C. near Charlotte, N. C.

Polk Monument. *Three hundred people attended the 1904 ceremony and unveiling which praised James K. Polk's presidency of the United States, an era which saw the admission of Texas, Iowa, and Wisconsin as states; the establishment of the U.S. Naval Academy and Smithsonian Institution; and the acquisition of upper California and New Mexico. This monument marks the first residence of Polk (1795–1849) eleven miles south of Charlotte at 308 South Polk Street in Pineville, not Fort Mill, South Carolina, as stated on the postcard. The monument was originally placed by the Daughters of the American Revolution, Mecklenburg Chapter, as the first in North Carolina dedicated to Polk's memory. In 1966, the monument pictured was dismantled and reassembled nearby on the acreage of Polk's 250-acre family farm, which the family had left when they migrated to Tennessee in 1806. The twenty-two-acre site was acquired for a North Carolina State Historic Site by the Division of Archives and History, which created the James K. Polk Memorial with a museum-visitor center and a furnished, full-scale reproduction of the 1795 Polk homestead.*

Postcard publishers in the early 1900s looked for ingenious ways to increase sales. Seasonal greeting postcards were popular, especially for Christmas, Thanksgiving, and Valentine's. One Christmas gimmick, called puzzle cards, created four cards, one to be sent each of the four days before Christmas, showing parts of a Santa scene. The last card had Santa's face and revealed finally what was in his pack! Some illustrated novelty cards were birth announcements, and Rally Day or Reward cards to encourage attendance at Sunday School. Pennant cards were popular, too, such as these whimsical cards which added a pennant flag with the name of a town, state, person, or greeting. A whole array of novelty cards became available in America showing demure but titillating naughty ladies who revealed their bare arms, neck, and shapely, stocking-clad ankles.

SELECTED BIBLIOGRAPHY

Manuscript and Archival Sources

Charlotte-Mecklenburg Historic Landmarks
  Commission
  Survey and Search Reports
"Copy of Old Specifications of Mecklenburg County
  Courthouse," Cleveland County, N.C., July 30,
  1842 (copy given to Martin Boyer Jr. by Hannah
  Withers)
J. Murrey Atkins Library, Special Collections,
  University of North Carolina at Charlotte
  "Mecklenburg Library," 1771 (copy made from
    the N.C. mss. in the Dr. Francis L. Hawks
    Collection, New-York Historical Society, New
    York, N.Y.)
"The Johnston Building" (Charlotte: Honeycutt
  Printing Co., n.d.) (brochure in possession of
  Mary Boyer)
"Mecklenburg County Building Permits," 1911–85,
  microfilm
Mecklenburg County Register of Deeds Office
  Deed Books
National Register of Historic Places
  Information System for Mecklenburg County
North Carolina Division of Archives and History,
  Department of Cultural Resources, Raleigh
  Polk, Thomas, Estate Papers, Mecklenburg
    County, N.C., 1794
Public Library of Charlotte and Mecklenburg
  County
  Robinson-Spangler Carolina Room
    "American Trust Company," 1951
"Celebrating a Century of Service at the
  Public Library of Charlotte and
  Mecklenburg County, 1891–1991"
"Central Hotel," 1901
"Charlotte Memorial Hospital: Highlights
  of the Hospital's History" (Cleveland,
  Tenn.: Hospital Publications, 1969)
"Commercial National Bank," 1949
"Elmwood Cemetery Records," Charlotte, N.C.,
  beginning 1853, microfilm
Sanborn Insurance Maps of Charlotte, microfilm
U.S. Census Records, microfilm
Vertical files

Books

Abbott, F. C. *Fifty Years in Charlotte Real Estate,
  1897–1947.* Charlotte: Privately published, 1947.
Alexander, Julia. *Charlotte in Picture and Prose.*
  Charlotte: Privately published, 1906.
Andrews, Mildred Gwin. *Men and the Mills.* Macon:
  Mercer University Press, 1987.
Art Work of Charlotte. Chicago: Gravure Illustration
  Co., 1905.
Art Work of Piedmont Section of North Carolina.
  Chicago: Gravure Illustration Co., 1924.
Beaty, Mary D. *A History of Davidson College.*
  Davidson: Briarpatch Press, 1979.
Bishir, Catherine W. *North Carolina Architecture.*
  Chapel Hill: University of North Carolina Press,
  1990.
Bishir, Catherine W., Charlotte V. Brown, Carl R.
  Lounsbury, and Ernest H. Wood III. *Architects
  and Builders in North Carolina: A History of the
  Practice of Building.* Chapel Hill: University of
  North Carolina Press, 1990.
Blythe, LeGette, and Charles Raven Brockmann.
  *Hornets' Nest: The Story of Charlotte and
  Mecklenburg County.* Charlotte: McNally of
  Charlotte, 1961.
Boyte, Jack O. *Houses of Charlotte and Mecklenburg
  County.* Charlotte: Delmar Printing, 1992.
Bradbury, Tom. *Dilworth: The First 100 Years.*
  Charlotte: Dilworth Community Development
  Association, 1992.
*Charlotte, North Carolina: Diversified, Industrial and
  Commercial Center.* Charlotte: Observer Printing
  House, 1927.
Claiborne, Jack. *"The Charlotte Observer": Its Time
  and Place, 1869–1986.* Chapel Hill: University of
  North Carolina Press, 1986.
———. *Jack Claiborne's Charlotte.* Charlotte:
  Charlotte Publishing, 1974.
*Cyclopedia of Eminent and Representative Men of
  the Carolinas in the Nineteenth Century.* Vol. 2.
  Madison, Wis.: Brant and Fuller, 1892.
Dowd, Clement. *Life of Vance.* Charlotte: Observer
  Printing House, 1897.
Dowd, Jerome. *Sketches of Prominent Living North
  Carolinians.* Raleigh: Edwards and Broughton,
  1888.
Eppley, Frances Fielden. *First Baptist Church of
  Charlotte.* Charlotte: Heritage Printers, 1981.

Fetters, Thomas T., and Peter Swanson Jr. *Piedmont and Northern: The Great Electric Interurban System of the South*. San Marino, Calif.: Golden West Books, 1947.

Graham, George W. *Mecklenburg Declaration of Independence*. Charlotte: Queen City Printing and Paper Co., 1898.

Greenwood, Janette. *On the Homefront: Charlotte during the Civil War*. Charlotte: History Department of the Mint Museum, 1982.

——. *Presbyterian Hospital: The Spirit of Caring*. Dallas, Tex., 1991.

Hamilton, George, ed. *William H. Peeps, A.I.A.* Charlotte: Privately published, 1928.

Hanchett, Thomas W. *Sorting Out the New South City: Race, Class, and Urban Development in Charlotte, 1875–1975*. Chapel Hill: University of North Carolina Press, 1998.

Harkey, H. Hugh, Jr. *Greetings from Charlotte: A Pictorial Postcard History of Charlotte*. Hornet's Nest Productions, 1992.

Harris, Wade. *Sketches of Charlotte*. Charlotte: Hirst Printing Co., 1888.

——. *Sketches of Charlotte*. Charlotte: Observer Printing House, 1896.

——. *Sketches of Charlotte*. Charlotte: Ray Printing Co., 1907.

——. *Sketches of Charlotte*. Charlotte: Observer Printing House, 1924.

Hearden, Patrick J. *Independence and Empire*. DeKalb, Ill.: Northern Illinois University Press, 1882.

Hook, C. C., and F. M. Sawyer. *Some Designs by Hook and Sawyer*. Charlotte: Queen City Printing and Paper Co., 1902.

Kratt, Mary Norton. *Charlotte: Spirit of the New South*. Tulsa, Okla.: Continental Heritage Press, 1980.

——. *Charlotte: Spirit of the New South*. 2d ed. Winston-Salem, N.C.: John F. Blair, 1992.

Kratt, Mary Norton, and Thomas Hanchett. *Legacy: The Myers Park Story*. Charlotte: The Myers Park Foundation, 1986.

Lafferty, Robert H. *History of the Second Presbyterian Church, 1873–1947*. Charlotte: The Herald Press, 1953.

——. *The North Carolina Medical College, Davidson and Charlotte, North Carolina*. Charlotte: Privately published, 1946.

Lockman, Barbara B. *A Century's Child: The Story of Thompson Children's Home, 1886–1986*. Charlotte: Thompson Children's Home, 1986.

McEwen, Mildred. *First United Methodist Church*. Charlotte: Heritage Printers, Inc., 1982.

——. *Queens College Yesterday and Today*. Charlotte: Heritage Printers, Inc., 1980.

Marsh, Kenneth, and Blanche Marsh. *Charlotte: Carolinas' Queen City*. Columbia, S.C.: R. L. Byron, 1967.

Maschal, Richard. *Wet-Wall Tattoos*. Winston-Salem, N.C.: John F. Blair, 1993.

Massengill, Stephen E., and Robert M. Topkins. *A North Carolina Postcard Album*. Raleigh: N.C. Department of Cultural Resources, 1988.

Milburn, Frank P. *The Work of Frank P. Milburn, Architect, Charlotte NC*. Charlotte: Queen City Printing and Paper Co., 1899.

Mitchell, Miriam Grace, and Edward Spaulding Perzel. *The Echo of the Bugle Call: Charlotte's Role in World War I*. Charlotte: Heritage Printers, Inc., 1979.

Morgan, Hal, and Andreas Brown. *Prairie Fires and Paper Moons: The American Photographic Postcard: 1900–1920*. Boston: David R. Godine, 1981.

North Carolina Year Book and Business Directory. Raleigh: News and Observer Publishing Co., 1914.

Pope, Sarah Manning, and Emily Newman Weil. *Postcards of Old Wayne County, NC*. Goldsboro: Wayne County Historical Association, 1995.

Powell, William S., ed. *Dictionary of North Carolina Biography*. Vols. 1–6. Chapel Hill: University of North Carolina Press, 1979–94.

Preyer, Norris W. *Hezekiah Alexander and the Revolution in the Backcountry*. Charlotte: Heritage Printers, Inc., 1987.

Reynolds, D. R., ed. *Charlotte Remembers*. Charlotte: Community Publishing Co., 1972.

Romine, Dannye. *Mecklenburg: A Bicentennial Story*. Charlotte: Independence Square Associates, 1975.

St. Martin's Chapel: A Brief History of Its Origin and Work, 1887–1937. Charlotte: Lassiter Press, 1937.

Shaw, Cornelia Rebekah. *Davidson College*. New York: Fleming H. Revell Press, 1923.

Smith, Mrs. S. L., comp. *North Carolina's Confederate Monuments and Memorials*. Raleigh: Edwards and Broughton Co., 1941.

Stautzenberger, Anthony J. *The Establishment of the Charlotte Branch Mint: A Documented History*. Austin, Tex.: N.p., 1976.

Strong, Charles M. *History of Mecklenburg County Medicine*. Charlotte: News Printing House, 1929.

Thompson, Edgar. *Agricultural Mecklenburg and Industrial Charlotte, Social and Economic*. Charlotte: Queen City Printing Co., 1926.

Tompkins, D. A. *History of Mecklenburg County and the City of Charlotte from 1740 to 1903*. Charlotte: Observer Printing House, 1903.

Unveiling of the Monument to the Signers of the Mecklenburg Declaration of Independence, May 20, 1898. Charlotte: Observer Printing House, 1898.

Weaver, C. E. (Illustrated Cities Series). *Story of Charlotte*. Privately published, 1913.

Wilkinson, Henrietta. *The Mint Museum of Art at Charlotte*. Charlotte: Heritage Printers, Inc., 1983.

Williams, Elizabeth. *A History of the First Presbyterian Church, 1821–1983*. Charlotte: Heritage Printers, Inc., 1983.

Winston, George Tayloe. *A Builder of the New South: Being the Story of the Life Work of Daniel Augustus Tompkins*. New York: Doubleday, Page and Co., 1920.

Withey, Henry F., and Elsie Rathburn Withey. *Biographical Dictionary of American Architects (Deceased)*. Los Angeles: Hennessey and Ingall, 1970.

Wright, Christina, and Dan Morrill, eds. *The Charlotte-Mecklenburg Historic Driving Tour.* Charlotte: Metrographics, 1993.

Periodicals, Pamphlets, and Directories

Alexander, Violet. "The Confederate States Navy Yard at Charlotte, N.C., 1862–1865." *The North Carolina Booklet,* Jan., Apr., July, Oct. 1926, pp. 29–37.

Around City Hall. Charlotte, N.C., Jan. 1978, vol. 5, no. 6.

Boyer, M. E., Jr. "Mecklenburg County Courthouse." *Southern Architect and Building News* 54, no. 10 (Oct. 1928): 57–61.

Bridges, Daisy Wade. "The Mint Museum of Art— Then and Now." *Antiques and Collecting,* June 1986, pp. 80–84.

Carolina Architecture and Allied Arts, Miami, Fla., 1940 ed.

Carolina Pythian 10, no. 5 (souvenir edition, 1905).

Catawba Journal

Charlotte Chronicle

Charlotte City Directory, 1884–present

Charlotte Daily Observer

Charlotte Journal

Charlotte Observer

"Historic Sites (James K. Polk Memorial)." *Carolina Comments* 46, no. 4 (July 1996): 84–85.

McInness, Frank G. "The First N.C. Skyscraper." *The State* 51, no. 5 (Oct. 1983): 14–17.

Myers, John Quincy, M.D. (Tranquil Park Sanitarium). "The Natural Instincts in Relation to Disease and Psychoses." *Charlotte Medical Journal* 76, no. 3 (Sept. 1917): 146.

"Official Program: 39th Annual Reunion United Confederate Veterans." Charlotte: Published in Honor of the Thinning Ranks of Gray, June 4–7, 1929.

People's Paper

Piedmont Builders (New Orleans, La., n.d.)

Prominent Builders of the Carolinas. Mount Vernon, N.Y.: Architects Publishing Co., n.d.

Telephone Directory, Charlotte, 1922–present

INDEX